Careers Without College

No B.S. Necessary

Jo Ann Oritt Russo

Betterway Publications, Inc.
White Hall, Virginia

41222

Published by Betterway Publications
White Hall, VA 22987

Cover Design by David Wagner

Copyright © 1985 by Jo Ann Oritt Russo

Library of Congress Cataloging-in-Publication Data

Russo, Jo Ann,
    Careers without college.

    Bibliography: p.
    Includes index.
    1. Vocational guidance — United States. 2. High school graduates — Employment — United States. I. Title
HF5382.5.U5R88 1985   331.7′023′0973   85-30713
ISBN 0-932620-60-4 (pbk.)

Printed in the United States of America
0 9 8 7 6 5 4 3 2

Contents

To Carl

Introduction

It is not the purpose of this book to advise anyone to continue or not continue their formal education. However, a very large factor in the decision will naturally be your career goals, and that is where the book can help.

There is more to college than academics, of course. Classroom education is but one part of the total college experience. Even within the educational spectrum, there is more to consider than may be evident at first glance.

For the purposes of this book, we will examine the value of education from an institution offering specialized curricula; i.e., majors in such disciplines as Business, Computer Science and/or Finance. The reason is that, while it is still possible to pursue a very general degree in Liberal Arts from select small colleges, the vast majority of students entering college today do not go this route. They opt rather for a "practical" bachelor's degree, for one reason. They believe that only such a degree will open the door to exciting and lucrative careers. Well, it ain't necessarily so.

From an employer's perspective, there are several advantages to hiring someone with a college degree. The first is simply that on the surface, there appears to be less risk involved in hiring the degreed candidate. By all rights, you should be a blinding success; after all, you have a degree. Certainly the poor slob who hired you knows he is above reproach, which is precisely why he hired you. He made the safe play.

Sometimes you will encounter the exalted Company Policy (carved in granite) which states that a college degree *or equivalent experience* is required to be considered for the position you want. But the operative phrase here is "or equivalent experience." All of the careers in this book with the exception of nursing are open to those with equivalent experience, and indeed, many employers prefer such experienced candidates to degreed ingenues.

Finally, it is possible that an employer might prefer a degreed candidate because of his or her education. It sounds odd put that way, but that is in fact one of the least likely reasons for bias toward degreed applicants. After all, very few first jobs, whether the new employee is just out of high school or law school, carry with them much real responsibility. Your most valuable education will be what comes after, not before you are hired.

College, then, does not fully prepare one for a career. At best, it may be useful in landing a job. This benefit is not without a price. Recent studies project that the class of 1991 (today's high school juniors) will pay an average of $35,000 for a sheepskin from a *public* university. A private college education will run about twice that. That's a pretty expensive résumé-builder, especially when you consider that instead of *paying* that amount, you could be *earning* it.

Let's consider the cases of two high school students graduating in 1987. Both are interested in careers in data processing. Student A reasearches which colleges have the best Computer Science programs. He applies. He is accepted. He spends four years studying computers. He graduates. He gets a programming job paying $20,000 a year. Years later he emerges from debt, a changed man.

Student B, on the other hand, has the luck to be turned down for student aid. She gets a job as a computer operator earning $13,000 a year. Four years later she is $52,000 ahead (assuming no raises.) But more importantly, she now has four solid years of computer experience, and is probably ready for promotion to a programming position. Very likely she will be competing with Student A for the next job up the data processing career ladder. You'd better believe my money's on Student B.

All of this is not to say that you could not benefit from having a college education. Many (but not all) people at the very top of their professions have college backgrounds. These examples have been given primarily to illustrate that there are alternatives which can make a lot of sense, especially considering that, once you have started on your career path, you can probably get the same education Student A mortgaged his grandmother for without paying tuition.

Fully 75% of the Fortune 500 companies offer their employees some form of tuition assistance. Many smaller companies do, too. In many cases, college courses cost the employee absolutely nothing. Even if you must pay part of the cost, it is always less than half the total, *and you are earning a good salary as you go.*

This examination of the costs and benefits of a college education is meant to at least give you pause to consider the alternatives and options available to you. I am not, however, unaware that, for many students, education is but one (perhaps trace) element of Going to College. Let's now consider the College Experience.

Anyone who has seen the movie *Animal House* has a pretty good idea of what college life is supposed to be like — wild parties, torrid romance and food fights. More serious students imagine afternoons in ivy-covered buildings spent contemplating deep and meaningful questions of life and art. I have some terrible news.

Bluto and his friends wouldn't last two weeks in any college or university in the country. Neither would Plato. The real college experience is likely to consist of rote learning of material taught by graduate assistants in an atmosphere of intense competition and tremendous pressure. You can rarely get into the courses you want or pass the ones you get into. Your roommate catches every disease that sweeps the campus, and passes it on to you. You would have made the Dean's list last term except for Economics, in which that twisted cretin of a professor gave you a D. Your parents will not shell out $12,000 a year for D's, as they are constantly reminding you. And what will you do with a degree in Economics, anyway?

Of course, this is a pointedly bleak picture of college life, though not without some truth, and there are certainly positive aspects of higher education not described here. And yet I believe most people are disappointed, to varying degrees, by their actual college experiences. This may be because few people at the age of 18 are in a position to make full use of much that college has to offer. Indeed, my own experience would have been immeasurably more satisfying had I delayed attending college a few years.

The decision not to attend college, should that be your choice at this time, is not like Faust's. You can always change your mind. It is an ever-growing phenomenon in America today that young adults and older people are dropping out of the work force to attend college and graduate schools. They bring with them so much more that they cannot help having richer and fuller experiences. They have not only a clearer focus on what they expect but a deeper appreciation for what they achieve. It is possible that you will wake one morning and deeply regret having not gone to college "when you had the chance.-"But you can make another choice — go, and you'll be glad you waited.

In the meantime, there are a great many exciting and financially rewarding careers for which you can be ready right now. The purpose of this book is to introduce you to ten such careers, explain what they are all about, where they can lead and how to prepare for them. As stated earlier, none of these careers requires a college degree. In some cases, such as commercial art, other training may be desirable;

but the majority of fields discussed can be entered right out of high school.

It sometimes seems that everyone is eager to give young people all kinds of advice about school, work and life in general. Some advice can be very valuable; a lot must be taken with the proverbial grain of salt. But almost all of it concerns what you should do — where you *should* go to school, what companies you *should* apply to, what offers you *should* accept. A lot of this is premature at best, because most people really don't know what all their options are. Thus, I have absolutely no feelings one way or the other about what you *should* do, and the book is meant to reflect this objectivity. Read it. Sit down and think about what you *want* to do. Then do it.

The format of the book is designed to give you the information you need in the most useful and easily understandable way. You will notice that all of the chapters are organized along the same line. A brief overview of the profession is given first, followed by a description of typical entry-level jobs in the field, including responsibilities, compensation and work environment. Then various career paths are presented, as well as representative specialties one may choose to develop. Finally, practical ways to prepare for these careers (educationally and hands-on) are explored. Naturally, in real life, the preparation comes first, but here it is discussed at the end.

I would expect few people to have consuming interest in all of the careers presented here. More important, even fewer have enough information about career possibilities to decide if they are interesting or not. What do media buyers do? How much do mortgage loan officers make? How far can I go in data processing? These questions are answered in the beginning of the respective chapters. If, after the overview, you are interested in pursuing a particular career, you can read on and find out how to prepare for it.

And prepare you must. Although the careers in this book do not require a college degree, they are not grunt work, nor are the jobs lightly handed out. Careers without college can be exciting, lucrative and highly rewarding. They are also a lot of work. Not only are you a non-degreed candidate competing with hordes of eager college graduates, you are also years younger than your degreed counterparts. Employers will be harder to impress, and you must try harder to do so. If you are ready to take the challenge, read on.

1

Advertising

Some years ago, the Ronzoni spaghetti company ran a series of television commercials extolling the virtues of its product, chief among which was freshness. This freshness, they said, was due to the fact that Ronzoni spaghetti was harvested daily, and to prove it, the commercials showed groves of pasta trees from which Italian farm laborers picked only the best to bear the Ronzoni name. Much to the surprise of company executives, many letters were received from people pleased to learn at last that spaghetti grew on trees.

Naturally, most people recognized the humor in the Ronzoni commercial. Nonetheless, advertising in general affects more people in more ways than almost any other business in America today. It profoundly influences what we eat, wear, drive, watch, read, do and think. This influence is so pervasive that advertising personalities become celebrities, and Ronald McDonald is better known than the Attorney General of the United States. Almost everyone knows what is the real thing, where America shops and how to spell relief (think about that one). Yet catchy slogans and cute commercials are only the surface.

Of course, someone has to write the slogans (a copywriter) and lay out the art work (artists). But who decides where to run the ads? A lot of that depends on who is expected to buy the product. And who determines that? Who convinces the Pepsi people to contract with their agency in the first place? These are critical responsibilities, carried out by unsung heroes behind the scenes. Because advertising is a business as well as an art, the services of account executives, market researchers and media buyers are central to the success of any agency.

[13]

————————PEOPLE IN ADVERTISING————————

Basically, advertising agencies are divided into two areas: creative services and marketing. Within creative services, or production, are generally two groups, copywriters and artists. These two fields in particular welcome talented, ambitious individuals, and are little concerned with titles or degrees. Let's look first at copywriting.

Advertising copywriters, as the title implies, write copy. Writing ads is a lot like acting: it looks easy, and every man, woman and child in America thinks he or she can do it. But the trick is not only to think up catchy jingles and slogans, but to think up ones that will make a product sell. "Newlyweds and nearly deads" is cute and it rhymes, but it's not a slogan likely to fill rooms at a resort hotel. Copywriters work very closely with both their own and the clients' marketing people, trying to define the perfect image for a particular product. People buy things for all different reasons, some of them contradictory. The same person who buys TIDE laundry detergent ("America's favorite") drinks Fresca for that original taste. A copywriter tries to capture the essence of a product and convey that to a targeted audience.

Copywriters must also write ads that convey information. We all can remember those television commercials where a man and a woman seem to be forever running toward each other, yet never get any closer. We may even remember the slogan ("the closer you get, the better she looks"). But what product was being advertised? Better yet, what product did Josephine the plumber tout so highly? If people remember the ad but not the product, the ad is a flop.

Less exciting but just as important as creative brainstorming are client presentations. Although most selling is done by account executives, copywriters attend a great many meetings with clients, and must not only be prepared to explain (or defend) their work, but to change it, too. In today's litigious society, it is also important for a copywriter to avoid ethnic, sexist and racist stereotyping in their ads. It's doubtful the Frito Bandito would debut in an ad campaign today.

The copywriter's partner in creative crime is the commercial artist. Where the copywriter conveys a message with words, the artist speaks with pictures. In print advertising, for example, the artist is responsible for "laying out" the ad; i.e., drawing mechanicals, or "blueprints" of an ad to scale. But the larger job is designing the ad. What type of scene should the ad depict? How should the product be displayed? Artists agonize for days over what color shirt a model should wear. Should the model drink the product, or merely hold it?

What should be the overall tone of the ad? It is crucial that the copywriter and artist agree on these things, lest a client wind up with an ad featuring a Queen Elizabeth look-alike endorsing "the gas with guts."

Like the copywriter, the artist works closely with marketing people (his own and the client's) to present the right image to the desired audience. Even more than words, pictures can have many different meanings, and there truly is no accounting for taste. A client may want a "handsome" spokesman for his product. If the client is over the age of 50, he probably has in mind someone like Gregory Peck, and will be more than surprised to find John Travolta extolling Wonder Pop. And yet many potential Wonder Pop consumers may have never heard of Gregory Peck.

And finally, while it may be true that one must suffer for art, one cannot make the client suffer too much, at least not financially. Your idea of the perfect Wonder Pop ad might be a 60 second commercial spot (during the SuperBowl) featuring the cast of *Grease* dancing through Buckingham Palace. Wonder Pop's advertising budget may force you to settle for the boss's daughter walking through the plant. Both can be effective. It is up to the artist to design successful ads in all media for all budgets.

Behind the scenes in advertising toil those faceless pros of the business: the marketing people. Some areas of statistical research do require specialized education, though not at the entry level. But the two general groups of marketing professionals, researchers and account executives, welcome talented and ambitious non-degreed applicants. First let's consider research.

Through consultation with a client, market researchers determine the target consumer group(s) for a particular product. For example, a client may feel that his cereal, Chestnut Bark, should be marketed primarily to "health conscious people." The market researcher will try to define "health conscious" demographically; that is, the kinds of people likely to be health conscious. Many statistical studies and tools are used in the analysis, and a consumer base is identified. It may be found that Chestnut Bark has high appeal to young, married professionals earning over $30,000 a year who live in the western half of the United States.

The market researcher then searches for any and all information about that target group. Where do they vacation? Do they have children? Pets? Bad teeth? How often do they eat out? Go bowling? Get a haircut? What sports do they play and watch? What celebrities do they admire? Whom do they dislike? To what political party do they belong? What civic groups? Do they donate blood? All significant correlations are noted, and the information is discussed with the creative team to help set the tone for the ad campaign. It may well be that a tattooed man chewing tobacco will not sell much Chestnut Bark, particulary if the ads are run in *Guns and Ammo* magazine. Which brings us to the second half of market research; namely, deciding where the client will get the most response for his advertising dollar.

What do young married professionals earning over $30,000 a year and living in the western half of the country read? What do they watch? When? These things are determined by a specialized type of researcher called a media buyer. Media buyers research advertising markets the way market researchers research consumer markets. All kinds of statistical data about magazine, newspaper, radio and television audiences are available, and media buyers use such data to allocate the client's resources. In fact, a lot of media advertise in their own arenas; for instance, those full-page ads in *Philadelphia Magazine* claiming "47% of our readers traveled abroad last year," or "*Philadelphia Magazine* subscribers spent an average of $1560 on pet care products last year." If jet-setting animal lovers are identified as health conscious, the makers of Chestnut Bark might do well to consider advertising in that publication.

The other marketing professionals in advertising are the account executives, or salespeople. Advertising salespeople are different than people who sell retail goods, and even from other service salespeople. It has never really been shown that advertising has a measurable effect on product sales. An account executive cannot therefore go door-to-door selling a product or service in the same sense other industry salespeople do. Most often, account executives preach to the converted, selling their agencies' services to companies who already advertise through competing agencies.

The single largest job of account executives — before the sale, at least — is learning about, preparing for and winning advertising competitions. Such competitions are held regularly when a client is considering a change in agency representation. First, an account executive must convince the company to allow his agency to bid on the campaign. Of all those wishing to compete, perhaps no more than ten firms are chosen to present material. These firms are chosen primarily on the basis of their work for other clients. Once the final group of competitors is selected, the real work begins.

The account executive, with the help of the creative team, determines the approach. Should they submit a series of print ads, or taped TV commercials? Should the ads follow the general tone of the client's previous campaigns, or should they cut a bold, new stroke? How much should be spent (non-reimbursed) to get the account? How much will it be worth if the agency lands it? Who else is competing? What approach is the competition likely to take? This process can take months of twelve-hour days, seven days a week. The successful account executive must pick and choose those competitions in which his firm has a good chance of winning, so that resources are not continually wasted.

Once an account has been won, the account executive serves as a liaison between his client and the agency. He is the contact person for clients, who communicate to him their plans to introduce new products, expand into new markets, etc. A good account executive will not be satisfied with just landing an account. It is well and good that Wonder Pop's television commercials and print ads are produced by his firm. But what about packaging? Perhaps a new logo would attract consumers. And what about the Wonder Flake laundry product division of the company? An account executive should use his "foot in the door" to expand his agency's business within existing accounts, as well as go after new ones.

As we have seen, there are many diverse and exciting types of careers in advertising. Even more encouraging is the fact that though you will not start at the top, the entry level need not be dull. Let's look at some typical entry level jobs and responsibilities.

———————— THE ENTRY LEVEL ————————

On the creative side, copywriters usually begin as editors. In many agencies, the title "editor" is really a euphemism for go-fer, because editing is not really a full-time job. In between, you could find yourself typing presentations, preparing direct mail advertising, taking notes in meetings with clients, and generally doing menial jobs that need to be done. This will all be terrific experience, as well as expose you to many different aspects of the advertising business. This is important, because though you may only be interested in, say, copywriting, you will not work in a vacuum, and are certain to fail miserably without a good understanding of and appreciation for everything else involved in making an agency successful.

Advertising artists almost always begin on a paste-up and layout staff, handling the routine details of art production. These include preparing mechanical drawings of print ads, laying out photo ads, "pasting up" or preparing work for the camera, outfitting commercial models and so on. Like editing, paste-up and layout experience gives advertising artists a broad background from which to develop one or more of many specialties later on. It is also the best way to build a portfolio of produced work, which will be useful should you decide to change jobs.

Marketing is probably the easiest area of advertising to break into. Initially, you might work for a magazine or radio station selling advertising space/time to agencies and corporations. This will introduce you to the "movers and shakers" of the advertising world, who will be valuable contacts to have later in your career. You may also move into market research for a medium — for example, *The Wall Street Journal.* Recently, the *Journal* has begun advertising itself in its own pages, proclaiming that "68% of Fortune 500 company CEO's subscribe to *The Wall Street Journal.*" How do they know that? Because some enterprising soul did the research, designed a questionnaire, researched and purchased mailing lists, tabulated the results and correlated the data with the *Journal*'s readership. This is a great way to gain experience useful to your agency research or media buying career.

Advertising can be a lucrative as well as exciting field. Entry-level copywriters can expect to earn between $13,000 and $16,000 a year to start. Within three years, that figure jumps to $24,000 or more. Advertising artists are often hired on a free-lance basis to start, and are paid hourly or by the job. It should work out to at least $13,000 a year. A permanent full-time position should definitely pay that much. With two or three years' experience, an artist can command $20,000 a year, or $20 an hour as a free-lancer.

On the marketing side, ad space/time salespeople should earn salary and commission totalling $15,000 or so to begin. Experienced marketing people, in media or agency work, can make up to $30,000 after three or four years. There are very few entry-level market researchers. Usually, you work your way into the job, and thus have some relevant experience when you "start out." Expect to earn $18,000 or so initially. After a few years, market researchers and media buyers are paid $27,000 and up.

The work environment in an ad agency is unique. Everything hinges on winning and keeping clients, and there can be a lot of pressure to perform, particularly for those on the creative team. On the other hand, a job well done is rewarded quickly and handsomely, and it is unlikely that the lack of a degree will have much effect on your career. You are free to rise or fall by yourself. To some this is an exciting challenge. But is also means there are no excuses, and you are only as good as your last campaign.

Like other "creative" businesses, advertising offers something beyond the usual nine-to-five grind. It is an exciting, fast-paced industry which tolerates a bit of eccentricity, recognizing that art needs freedom to develop. Hours can be flexible, though everyone, artiste or no, is expected to give his all when deadlines close in. Also like other creative businesses, it is a *business*. While the client may demand "only the best," a sharp eye is kept on costs, especially those which cannot be billed to an account. Competition is fierce, and profits most definitely count.

Finally, advertising is not for everyone. If you are the sort of person who performs best when given clear direction and few choices, you will be unhappy in the unstructured atmosphere of an ad agency. If you are prone to giving those responsible for an interesting but failed project "an A for effort," you will not last long in advertising. And if you are looking for just a job, avoid advertising altogether.

If, however, you are excited by the challenge of working with ideas, there are many different advertising career paths from which to choose. Let's look at the development of some typical advertising careers, what they demand and what they pay.

CAREER PATHS

The vast majority of advertising professionals work for advertising agencies. Though some large corporations do have internal advertising departments, they usually are represented by one or more agencies as well. Careers in advertising, then, are largely agency careers, so we will examine these first.

Some typical job titles in ad agencies include Art Director, Senior Writer, Producer, Creative Director, Account Executive and Media Buyer. Normally, an advertising artist will begin in layout, move into ad design, perhaps art production, and finally become Art Director. We have already examined entry-level layout responsibilities. What's next? The answer is ad design.

Once you have mastered the technical skills involved in mechanical drawing and paste-up, your next step is designing complete ads. At this point, it is important to avoid becoming too specialized. It is far too early in your career to limit yourself to designing only print ads, for example. It would be useful to also get experience in designing outdoor advertising, video commercials and perhaps packaging. You should be prepared to spend four to six years designing all different types of ads, with increasing creative responsibility as you go. Eventually, you will have assigned accounts for which you will have total artistic responsibility. A highly talented advertising artist will attract a loyal clientele, and should he ever wish to change jobs, his clients will probably follow him.

The top position in advertising art is Art Director. All advertising is supervised and approved by this individual, who is responsible not only for the creative departments, but also scheduling commercial tapings, meeting deadlines and working within a budget. An Art Director will have ten or fifteen years' experience in all phases of production and a good understanding of copywriting. He will work long hours and be handsomely rewarded. Top Art Directors command $60,000 a year and more, and the good ones are worth it.

The parallel career path in writing begins with editing, progresses through copywriting and up to Executive Writer, or Senior Writer. As we have said, editing is more of an introduction to agency procedures than actual writing experience. Thus, once you enter copywriting, expect to spend at least four or five years writing print ad slogans, radio jingles and TV commercial scripts. Again, try to expose yourself to as many media and accounts as possible. Consider writing direct mail pieces, billboard ads and promotional items (how about a Wonder Pop cooler?). As you gain experience, you will be given specific account responsibilities. Working closely with artists and producers, you will feel the excitement of seeing your images take shape and your ideas become reality. As a copywriter, you can expect your work to be more widely read than Shakespeare's!

Eventually, you may work your way up to Executive Writer. In this position, you will be responsible for doing the actual writing for only a few very important accounts. Principally, you will collaborate with clients and Art Directors to create a product's "image." You will make decisions concerning commercial scripts such as dialogue versus narration. Most important, you will oversee the copywriters to insure that their entire campaigns present consistent and well-integrated product images. For these services, you can expect to earn $35,000 to $45,000 a year or more.

Supervising both Art Directors and Writers is the Creative Director, who holds the highest ranking creative position. Contrary to the title, however, most Creative Directors have little involvement in creating ads. They primarily direct the activities of artists and writers, assign account responsibilities, review the results, make hiring and promotion decisions, schedule the agency's production time and personnel, and plan and implement budgets. Creative Directors are really commanding officers, marshalling their agency's resources to the most profitable ends. As usual, the generals are well paid. Creative Directors in top agencies can earn well over $100,000 a year. Even this is sometimes not enough to keep the best people, and because they have loyal clients and a lot of contacts in the business community, when they leave to start their own agencies, they take these people and their money with them.

Another career option to consider is free-lancing. If you are a creative free spirit, as many talented ad artists and copywriters are, you may feel too constrained by the limitations of permanent full-time agency work. Once you have gained some experience and developed a marketable portfolio, you can do very well working on a free-lance basis. Consider contracting not only with agencies, but directly with advertisers as well. Talented artists in particular have little difficulty keeping busy, working at jobs such as direct mail advertising design, preparing product bulletins, creating logos and designing trade show sets and materials. There is a lot to be said for the free-lance lifestyle, not the least of which is an attractive income, with rates of $20-$25 an hour not uncommon.

On the marketing side, we have shown how aspiring account executives often begin in advertising sales. After a few years there, a strong candidate may use his or her industry contacts to land an agency position. To start, you will probably be assigned to manage several existing accounts, and be given a geographical area or industry segment to "prospect," or canvas for sales. You will assist senior account executives in the preparation of audition campaigns. Over a period of three to five years, an account executive will gradually assume more responsibility, develop his own account base, service those accounts, etc., thus increasing the agency's business. Though easily overlooked, the account executive is a vital member of the agency team. Indeed, without the account executives' efforts, there would be no clients, and without clients, no agency.

Account executives, like salespeople in other industries, are compensated with a combination of salary and commission payments. Although the proportions and amounts vary from one firm to another, an experienced account executive should earn between $35,000 and $60,000 a year all told. Savvy advertising account executives are highly prized, and assiduously courted by rival agencies.

Equally important to an agency's success are market researchers and media buyers. These people pursue very technical careers in which they work with a lot of complex statistical analytical tools and survey methodology. Although it is possible to get into market research without advanced education, it is almost certain that you will need to study advanced mathematics, numerical analysis, statistical research and computer technology. Initially, market research is concerned with studying statistical data and making relevant correlations between survey results and target audiences as well as target markets. Later on, researchers get involved in designing questionnaires, planning test marketing of products and making other applications of numerical analysis.

Media buyers perform a specialized function within the research field, namely the study and analysis of advertising markets. Given finite resources (even GM's pockets are not bottomless) it is up to the media buyer to allocate resources where they will produce the greatest return. Once target audiences have been identified, it is no small task to determine how best to reach them. In some industries, direct mail advertising is most effective. For some products, print ads are best. Even with this decision made, the media buyer must choose the most appropriate medium to reach the audience and do a lot of price shopping and negotiating to strike the best deal. It is a fast-paced, high-pressure career in which millions of dollars are at stake every day. For performing under such conditions, researchers and buyers are well rewarded, earning between $35,000 and $50,000 a year with five or more years experience.

As mentioned previously, most advertising careers are with independent agencies. Many large companies, however, have in-house advertising departments, usually in addition to contracted agencies. Careers in corporate advertising are also exciting and rewarding, though somewhat different from those in agencies.

Corporate advertising departments can resemble small agencies, with some obvious exceptions. Naturally there are no account executives, though there is usually someone assigned to serve as liaison with the company's agencies. The creative team is comprised of artists and writers, just as in an agency. More often than in agencies, however, free-lance artists and writers are hired by the job. The work is also a bit different in nature.

Since most companies let their agencies do the bulk of the ad writing and production for their products, in-house people usually work on special projects, prepare artwork for their agencies to publish, or work in research (product managers). Of these jobs, the largest is certainly special events production and coordination.

Every industry has trade shows at which new products are introduced and a lot of selling is done. Corporate advertising people are responsible for their company's participation, from designing mobile displays and writing and preparing product data sheets and brochures to researching the competition, packaging the final product and surveying customer reaction. In addition to trade shows, the advertising department coordinates all kinds of special events such as participation in charity events, sponsoring Little League baseball teams and the like.

The scope of responsibilities of corporate "advertising" often includes public relations. This is an exciting field involving a lot of contact with media representatives, as well as salesmanship. A public relations representative is responsible for creating and maintaining a favorable and appropriate corporate image. Where advertising and promotions people may plan a celebrity/employee softball game for charity, it is up to the public relations director to solicit the participants, write press releases and get them in the paper. The major distinction of public relations is that it cannot be bought, like advertising space or time. The public relations person is constantly seeking new ways to keep the company's name and products before the public, and this involves a lot of selling, as well as catchy and positive news writing. Remember Tang?

SPECIALTIES

Even careers in "mainstream" advertising tend to become specialized. Most agencies as a whole develop special expertise in one area or another. The reason for this is simply that, in the highly competitive world of advertising, it is preferable to be master of one trade than jack of all and master of none. The same people who so successfully launched a disposable diaper campaign would be at a loss to create one for Boeing Vertol, and so you will find that agencies tend to specialize within industry groups such as consumer products, high-technology companies or business-to-business marketers.

In addition to specializing in advertising for particular industries, many agencies (and people) specialize in advertising through certain media. Some media specialties include direct mail, outdoor advertising, print, audio/video, promotional items and packaging. Most larger agencies will have separate departments that produce print and broadcast ads, and perhaps a direct-mail group. In the beginning, it's best to work in a diverse firm, and perhaps later move to a specialized agency. Indeed, such a move may be necessary, if you do not want to forever remain a little fish in a big pond. The manager of direct mail advertising with a large Madison Avenue firm is unlikely to become an agency vice-president, but his mail expertise will take him far with a direct mail specialty house.

It may be that no agency, whatever its size or focus, will hold your career interest for very long. Advertising is a field in which new ventures are begun daily. Many do not succeed, but many others do, and if you have a well-rounded background in advertising production and marketing, a client following and a bit of luck, there is no reason you shouldn't strike out on your own. Unlike other industries, such as banking or insurance, it is not crucial that you offer a "200 year tradition of service to the community." Brains, talent and guts have launched many a successful ad agency, and a fair percentage of founders have no degree higher than a diploma from the school of hard knocks. They are, however, prepared for the many challenges ahead, as are all successful advertising professionals. And so should you be.

———————— PREPARATION ————————

Preparation for a career in advertising can begin in high school. By far the most important courses will be English Composition and Writing. By English Composition, I am talking about good old-fashioned grammar and usage. While it seems that every high school with more than 100 students offers literature classes rivaling those taught at many universities, it is somehow out of fashion to care about spelling and syntax. Well, even if you have to learn it on your own, get to know your mother tongue.

Aside from the fact that any educated person should be able to put together coherent sentences and paragraphs, a good grasp of English syntax and grammar will be invaluable to your copywriting career, especially at the entry level. While it usually is assumed (often incorrectly) that degreed applicants are literate, you — as a non-degreed candidate — will have to prove it. Indeed, many agencies require proofreading and editing tests as conditions of employment. Idea man though you may be, you are far more likely to land your first job in advertising with strong basic English skills than with a brilliant campaign concept for "Dentu-Grab." Later in your career, your foundation in the language will reward you with the ability to express your thoughts clearly and directly (a rare talent, to judge from such slogans as "making machines do more so man can do more").

Once you have mastered the basics, you would be well served by taking creative writing and/or journalism courses. These classes should force you to organize a story effectively, communicate ideas concisely and take out three words where one will do. And yes, spelling counts. Try to avoid courses with little relevance like Poetry Appreciation and Short Verse. Journalism in particular is good experience; journalists must make their stories interesting enough to "sell" to newspapers. As a copywriter you also are in the selling business.

To prepare for a career in advertising art, take as many practical arts courses as possible. This includes shop. Most high schools offer design, drafting and wood shop classes. Take them. It is essential that you have a good background in scale drawing, layout, three-dimensional design and spacing. Be sure to keep prints of any drafting work you do on special projects. These can become part of your beginning portfolio.

Many schools also offer such fine arts courses as drawing, watercolor painting, sculpture, photography and crafts. By all means, take these too, being sure to include drawing. This is the single most important skill to master. I would also recommend courses in theater arts like costume design, make-up, lighting and set design (if they are offered). These will provide a good foundation for print and video ad production. Take pictures of your finished work from different angles and in different lighting conditions. Keep drawings of set designs and layouts, too.

Many people aspiring to advertising and other commercial art careers attend two year art schools, specializing in the commercial, or practical arts. These are excellent preparation for the kinds of things you will do at the entry level in advertising art. Most schools offer evening programs, and some agencies assist with tuition costs. Should you decide to take advantage of such a program, investigate what's available first. Be sure to find a school with a strong curriculum in the practical/commercial arts. Best would be those with faculty who work in the industry, as they are likely to be tuned into real job skills and requirements. They will also be great contacts to have once you graduate. Get written recommendations, and again, retain all finished work for your portfolio.

As for the marketing side of the business, there is not a lot to do educationally in preparation. Good communication skills are of course essential, so do take public speaking and English composition. Join the debating team, study business math and become familiar with at least one business computer language. For the most part, though, you can best prepare for advertising marketing through activities outside of the classroom.

The most obvious place to begin is your school yearbook, which offers the opportunity to gain experience in almost every aspect of advertising, from space sales to layout work. On the marketing side, get involved in selling space in the book to local companies. Sit down beforehand and think which companies would most benefit from such advertising. Make a case for advertising the particular products to the target audience (high school students). Be familiar with different ad sizes and rates, and keep a record of your activities.

The yearbook also needs people to lay out the artwork, draw logos, take pictures, develop and enlarge them and prepare camera ready art. Get involved in all of these areas. Again, keep copies. Another good arena in which to practice commercial art is production of school plays. Many skills, like costume design, make-up, prop selection, lighting and set design have close counterparts in advertising. Consider doing artwork for the playbill or selling space in it.

For prospective copywriters, the school newspaper offers a great opportunity to get valuable writing and editing experience. Look for new angles to familiar stories. Also try to write and print editorials in which you are "selling" a point of view. Editing will help you learn what makes one story better than another, and give you experience in clarifying an idea or position.

Beyond school activities, civic and community groups welcome volunteers to act as press agents. Somewhere in your town is a Moose Lodge, legal aid group, hospital volunteer society, boy scout troop or historical society eager for publicity. You can provide it. Attend group events. Take pictures or write a piece on the festivities. Make submissions to local newspapers. Not only will this be excellent experience, it also will help you make contacts in the business world. Then, too, you will get to know publishing people and procedures, and may land an entry level newspaper job.

It is not realistic to expect to work part-time in advertising while you are still in school. At best an artist might do a little free-lance work, but even that is not very likely without some experience. Most people, degreed or not, simply have to pound the pavement in search of that first agency job. It's a tough nut to crack, and getting into the right firm can take months of letters, phone calls, interviews and rejections. Don't get discouraged. Be persistent. Continue working for non-profit agencies or drama groups, Keep your portfolio and resume current. Practice your typing. Learn word processing. You're the Pepsi generation, and you deserve a break today. Be all that you can be.

2

Banking

After dentists, bankers probably are the most maligned group of professionals in American life. Bankers are portrayed as dull and heartless automatons, whose joy it is to foreclose on widows and orphans. They wear "bankers' gray" suits and work "bankers' hours," as we are all so quick to point out. Bankers are only too happy to see these misconceptions continue, as they discourage the hordes of eager job seekers sure to flood the banks were the truth to ever come out. It may be the best kept career secret today — that banking is maaahvelous!

The world of banking is the world of money. And who is not excited by money? Bankers are involved in every imaginable business transaction in which there is money to be made. Especially in recent years, with the passage of legislation allowing banks to expand their services, even the small town savings and loan is moving and shaking in high finance circles. Of course, the bread and butter of banking is still commercial and consumer lending, but now banks are extending their operations into money market investing, financial planning and brokerage services. Larger banks have entire departments devoted to ancillary banking services like IRA's, Keogh's and 401K plan investing. All of this translates into tremendous sums of money, and bankers control it.

And yet, unlike many fast-track industries, banking offers stable employment. While banks may be involved in high flying ventures, they are almost always sure to saddle another party with most of the risk. Yes, bad loans are written off, and yes, the banks lose money on them, but the high profit margins more than allow for such losses. Banking is a tremendously profitable business. For years, banks were able to borrow money (from depositors) at 5% interest, and lend it (to clients) at 10% and more. Sometimes the money was even free! I can't tell you how many people invested in Christmas and vacation clubs paying no interest at all. This is surely an extreme example of the secret of success in any business — buying low and selling high.

Aside from fantastic profitability, banks do not suffer from the same fluctuations in supply and demand that plague other industries. Because the supply of money is tightly regulated by the government, banks need not fear a money glut which might force their "selling price" downward. Similarly, the demand for money is regulated through fixing of interest rates (lower prices create more demand). Especially in the current economic climate, federal budget deficits alone assure a strong market for money. So do kitchen remodelings, trips to Hawaii, big ticket retail sales and the desire to own General Motors stock.

Most importantly for you, banking is a career in which there are many opportunities for non-degreed candidates. While some areas require advanced studies later on, it is very possible to start out with a high school diploma, a good mind for figures, a strong desire to succeed and a willingness to work hard.

Now that you're interested, let's look at what banking is all about. As you probably know, the $350 in your savings account is not actually sitting in a shoe box at the bank. It is helping to build a neighbor's house, send a classmate to cosmetology school or set up a new hardware store in business. You lend your money to the bank in exchange for a fixed rate of return, say 5%. Of course, if you were to try and borrow money from the same bank, you would find the price of money a bit higher, right now about 9-11%. The difference between these buying and selling prices is the bank's profit. That seems like a large profit, and it is, but it's not all gravy. Bad loans, poor management and insufficient funds in deposit can turn even those healthy margins into losses. That is where banking professionals come in.

—————————PEOPLE IN BANKING—————————

Basically, there are two types of core banking services — commercial and consumer. Commercial bankers service business accounts, providing loans, cash management services, investment advice, etc. Within commercial banking are two distinct fields — investment banking and commercial credit. Let's look briefly at investment banking.

I say briefly because this is not a likely career path for non-degreed candidates. In fact, even degreed applicants are apt to find their credentials inadequate for investment careers. Most investment bankers have graduate training in business and finance, as well as strong backgrounds in equities, bonds, debentures and other arcane instruments of investment. Investment bankers are responsible for advising large corporate clients on financial decisions involving hundreds of millions of dollars. They become highly specialized in particular industries. They are like gurus to their clients, who rely on them to advise not only what moves to make, but when and how much. This type of analysis and guidance requires in-depth knowledge of financial methods, securities laws, global economic trends and industry developments. Commercial credit, on the other hand, does not require advanced degrees or such sophisticated expertise.

Commercial credit officers are responsible for administering loans to business clients. Many people are under the impression that loan officers sit in the bank all day processing loans, deciding the fates of millions with a yea or nay. Indeed, anyone who has ever applied for a loan, business or otherwise, must certainly have come away with the idea that the loan officer had no interest one way or another in your basement refinishing plans. You only hoped he would deign to "approve" your "application" for the cash to do the job. Nothing could be further from the truth!

Like any other business, banks have a product to sell. Banks sell money. If they do not sell the money they have bought (from depositors), they do not make any profit. Soon they would go out of business. The most important responsibility of a commercial loan officer is to sell money (make loans). Certainly this involves a lot of paperwork, but the bank makes no money on that! Loan officers actively solicit customers, both at the bank and at client locations. Banks advertise heavily in business publications, hoping to attract choice accounts to their institutions. The commercial loan officer must bring in new accounts, evaluate risks, set up loans and otherwise take care of his customers. In banking, as in other industries, no customers means no business.

In most large banks, commercial credit is the largest money making activity. There may be many commercial loan officers in a single branch. Experienced commercial credit people are highly sought after, not only for their expertise, but their contacts as well. When loan officers change banks, so may a good many important accounts, and banks are careful to accommodate their top loan people.

On the other side of the coin is consumer banking. Basically, careers in consumer banking fall into one of two areas — consumer loan and bank administration.

Consumer loan officers are almost direct equivalents of commercial loan people, with the obvious difference that they service consumer, or individual accounts, rather than businesses. In addition, they usually sell a broader range of products, including not just direct loans, but also credit cards, IRA's, Certificates of Deposit, etc. Like their counterparts in commercial credit, consumer loan officers actively solicit business. They also advertise heavily, not only in newspapers and magazines, but on radio and television as well.

Within a consumer credit department there are usually two separate sub-departments — mortgage lending and personal loans. These are also known as secured and unsecured lending. That is, mortgage loans are "secured," or guaranteed, by the property being purchased. If you default on the loan, the bank simply takes back the house. With a personal loan, the bank is taking a greater risk. Though you usually must put up some collateral for the loan, it is still riskier than a mortgage loan, if only because there is no down payment to reduce the bank's liability. Consequently, rates are higher for personal loans than for mortgages.

Mortgage lending is the backbone of the local savings and loan. Mortgage loan officers must become familiar with local property values, title insurance regulations, FHA and VA mortgage requirements, settlement procedures and a myriad of other real estate transactions and practices. Many mortgage lenders are non-degreed professionals who have worked their way up in the bank. In truth, there is little value in degrees for most credit positions, as the knowledge and skills necessary to do the job are only acquired on the job. One cannot major in lending, and even if it were possible, a generalized lending degree would be of little use in an industry where familiarity with local property and procedures is of paramount importance.

The other key banking position is bank administrator. Banks with more than one location have managers and management staff at each branch. Such managers are responsible for all bank operations, including hiring, training and supervision of all bank employees, overseeing lending operations, customer service, reconciling total bank funds, and administering such miscellaneous bank services as brokerage services or IRA accounts. In addition, bank managers are charged with making a profit, just as loan officers are. Administrators, however, are concerned with generating deposit business, thus creating capital for the credit departments to sell.

Since the product banks sell is money, it stands to reason that they must have a source of supply. There are many such sources, but by far the cheapest, most plentiful and most common is depositors (business and individual). To attract depositors, bank administrators have many tools.

While administrators cannot play too much with actual interest rates, there are a great many other areas in which they have more flexibility. For example, some banks pay interest on checking accounts if a minimum balance is maintained. Others offer higher paying money market accounts with limited check writing privileges. All of these services are advertised prominently in every bank's best effort to attract your money.

Whether you are interested in consumer or commercial banking, credit or administration, you can be sure that there is plenty of opportunity at the entry level for aspiring non-degreed bankers. Many banks and other financial institutions offer in-house training programs. In any event, be prepared to take whatever is offered at the entry level, learn as much as possible on the job, and work your way up on your merits.

ENTRY LEVEL JOBS

A great many illustrious banking careers have begun at the tellers' window. What better place to learn what banking is all about? Tellers not only have a lot of interaction with customers, they must become familiar with all types of bank procedures and services, and are responsible for the proper handling of transactions involving very large sums of money. As a teller, you are the first line of defense against improperly credited or debited funds. Thus, tellers must always be conscientious about all the little details.

At the entry level, bank teller is not an overly lucrative position, considering the tremendous responsibility involved. Do not be surprised if you are offered no more than $11,000 or $12,000 to start. Frankly, this is because many people view being a bank teller as a good alternative to secretarial work, especially if they cannot type. There are an inordinate number of women in teller positions, both young girls waiting to marry and older women whose children are grown and like to keep busy (the women, not the children). Neither of these groups put much pressure on bank management to bring wages into line with the demands of the job. It is therefore up to you to make it clear that your interest in teller work is primarily as the first step up the banking career ladder. You should be reviewed at least every six months your first year, and you must press to be considered for higher level positions as they become available.

Another path upon which to begin your banking career is in credit as a loan processor. Processors work as assistants to loan officers, helping customers with paperwork, explaining procedures, answering phone inquiries, etc. This is an excellent beginning job, as it exposes you to all phases of the bank's credit operations. While you will not make any decisions about loan approvals at this level, your involvement with customers and loan paperwork will familiarize you with which types of loans are likely to be granted and which are not. You should begin to see patterns. You will learn about collateral, prior liens, liquid vs. fixed assets and other credit terminology. All of this will stand you in excellent stead as you progress into higher levels of credit operations.

Your responsibilities may, at first, seem little more than secretarial. You will type loan applications, make copies of financial statements, fill out forms and file reports with various bank committees and government financial agencies. You will answer phones and take messages for the loan officers. Gradually, however, you will be able to answer customer questions yourself. Don't just type reports, read them. If you don't understand something, look it up or ask. Learn the requirements of the various governmental credit agencies, so that you can screen unprepared applicants before they get to the loan officer's desk. Your industriousness will be noticed and rewarded.

As a beginning loan processor, you should expect to earn between $12,000 and $14,000. Again, this relatively low starting salary is typical of banking at the entry level, and you must fight for your due. Ask to be reviewed soon after hiring, and be sure your job performance merits a nice increase. If proper raises and promotions are not forthcoming after 18 months to two years, you may want to move to another bank where your skills and experience will be recognized.

A third entry level banking alternative is customer service. Customer service people have many and varied responsibilities, depending on the type of financial institution. At a savings and loan, you will be dealing primarily with individual customers, helping them to open new accounts, explaining different bank services and procedures, issuing travelers' checks, rolling over CD's and a myriad of other little jobs without which many people would revert to keeping their funds under their mattresses. In customer service at a larger commercial bank, you may become involved in processing pension plan investments, answering business account inquiries about different bank services, investigating disputed account charges, and generally keeping corporate customers happy with good old "Monolithic Bank and Trust — the bank that satisfies."

Entry level customer service positions pay about the same as other bank jobs to start out ($12-$14,000). However, for some unknown (at least to me) reason, customer service is considered more of a career position than is teller or loan processor. Customer service people are not clerks, they are representatives. They have their own phone extensions, inscribed memo pads and even business cards. It is a highly visible position. The most minor bank transaction requires the assistance of a customer representative, if only because they have the keys. Do well in customer service and you are on your way to a rewarding banking career.

Of course, there is more to any job than money or even responsibilities. Every career develops in a unique work environment, and banking is no exception. As I mentioned at the beginning of the chapter, many people envy bankers for working "bankers' " hours, that is 9:00 am to 3:00 pm. However, these are not actually bankers' hours, but *bank* hours. You will arrive well before 9:00 and work at least until 4:30. Many activities, such as reconciling the tellers' cash drawers, must be done before and/or after customers use the bank. Also, most banks are open late at least one evening per week, as well as Saturday morning. There is, however, a lot of truth to the rumor that every second Tuesday is a bank holiday. For example, banks in Pennsylvania are closed for Columbus Day. I'm not sure how universally this holiday is observed, but in Pennsylvania, it is.

Another peculiar thing about banking is that everyone is a vice president, or at least an assistant vice president (affectionately referred to as an AVP). This should not faze you. After two years on the job, you too may be one. It does, however, create a somewhat formal working atmosphere, and loan processors usually refer to the loan officer (a mere AVP), as "Mr. Carnegie," not Andy.

Above all, and for obvious reasons, banks strive to preserve their reputation as honest, safe and uncorruptible institutions of finance and the American way of life. It is no accident that we refer to a sure thing as "money in the bank." Banks depend on that image of strength and propriety. Indeed, where would we be if we didn't trust our Trusts? And so people who work in banking always must be above reproach. Usually those who actually handle cash are bonded, or investigated, before being hired. Overall, employees are encouraged to maintain a very professional atmosphere in the bank, especially during bank hours. Jokes about calling in sick from Brazil are frowned upon, and will do little to advance your career.

CAREER PATHS

As mentioned earlier, careers in banking follow two general paths, commercial and consumer banking. In commercial banking, we have seen how that part involved with investments and financial analysis generally is not an alternative for non-degreed applicants. Nonetheless, it is a vital banking function, and no discussion of the banking industry would be complete without some understanding of how banks invest.

I said before that investment analysts advise clients how to invest their money. They also advise the bank itself where to invest. A cursory review of any bank financial statement will reveal that the vast majority of bank assets are tied up not in home improvement loans but in IBM and Exxon. It's simple mathematics — borrow money at 5%, invest it in a 7% corporate bond. If the company develops financial problems, the investment may turn into a loss, which is why banks rarely invest in High-Flyers, Inc. If an IBM or GM goes south, we're all in trouble.

Because banks are accountable to their depositors as well as their shareholders, deciding how to invest bank funds is a tremendous responsibility. Many years of education and experience are required to make such decisions reasonably. Investment careers include bank financial analyst, corporate portfolio manager and investment adviser. On the other side of the commercial coin is commercial credit, which offers good career opportunities to hardworkers with no more than high school diplomas, good minds and sharp pencils.

If you start out as a loan processor, you should expect to spend two to three years learning the ins and outs of lending before advancing to loan officer (a position usually on the AVP level.) Loan officers solicit new customers, insure that loans and loan procedures comply with required regulations, evaluate collateralized assets, and sit on committees that decide in favor or against actually making loans. For these duties, you should receive between $20,000 and 29,000 a year. With 5-8 years experience as a lending officer, during which time you may have advanced to vice president, you are ready for promotion to Manager of Lending Operations.

The Manager of Lending Operations is responsible for all lending within a given banking region, usually including four or more bank branches. The Manager hires, trains, supervises and promotes (or fires) all lending personnel. In addition, he or she is responsible for meeting certain lending quotas, and maintaining a given level of profitability. Naturally, this requires them to perform a delicate balancing act between aggressively drumming up new loan business and carefully evaluating the downside risk of questionable loans. This requires a great deal of experience in all aspects of lending, and Managers of Lending Operations are well compensated, earning up to $50,000 in salary alone. Furthermore, most upper level bank positions include performance bonuses in the form of cash, profit sharing contributions and/or stock options. All in all, the rewards are very attractive.

In consumer banking, the career paths are equally rewarding. As in the commercial end, lending is a key area. Consumer loan officers have similar responsibilities to those of commercial lenders, except they service individual rather than business accounts. Naturally, individuals have different needs than corporations, and consumer loan officers must develop expertise in many different lending requirements and procedures.

Many banks have training programs specifically for consumer lending personnel. These are great if you can get into one, but if not, you will get as good or better experience processing loans for a couple of years. Once you move into a loan officer position (again, an AVP), you will be involved with appraising collateral property, advising customers about various government loan regulations, evaluating an applicant's credit worthiness, etc. Generally speaking, you should expect to spend four to six years in consumer lending before moving up to a vice president level position such as Mortgage Lending Supervisor, Portfolio Manager, or eventually, Manager of Lending Operations.

Another career path in consumer banking is bank administration. As we discussed earlier, most banks with multiple locations have local branch managers. Usually, experience for this position is gained through several years in customer service. At that point, you should be ready to tackle the responsiblities of bank branch management, and they are numerous and diverse. A bank manager has ultimate responsibility for all of the operations of their branch, including hiring and supervising all bank personnel in credit, customer service and clerical positions. They administer the various bank services, such as special accounts (IRA, brokerage), credit card applications and promotional programs. Bank managers have budgets for things like personnel, office supplies, computer time, etc. These budgets are directly related to profit margins, for which the manager is ultimately responsible.

Profits, in turn, are closely related to how much of its services a bank is able to sell, and at what price. In other words, to make money, banks must attract depositors. Thus, the most important job of a branch manager is bringing in money. To that end, managers advertise their banks' services and rates, solicit existing customers to open new types of accounts, offer investment assistance, and whatever else they can think of to do to make First National your bank.

For all of this, bank managers are paid between $27,000 and $38,000 a year with 5-7 years banking experience. Beyond that, top branch managers are promoted further to District Managers, Regional Directors and so on. At these levels, you can expect to earn $60,000 or more.

Outside of lending and administration, there are various bank services which offer career opportunities in consumer banking. Many banks, for example, now offer their customers brokerage services. Usually these are what are known as discount services, which offer primarily stock and bond quotes and transactions, but not investment advice. This path is discussed more fully in the next section on specialties. In addition to brokerage services, people in banking become product managers of such services as credit card accounts, certificates of deposit, and retirement accounts. Product managers generally work at bank headquarters, and report to managers in corporate marketing.

Marketing is an area of banking which is not easily subsumed by the commercial or consumer side. As in any other industry, banks have marketing departments, and they are responsible for promoting bank services and products at the corporate level. Usually, you will start out as an assistant product manager for a particular area; for example, personal loans. Initially, you will be involved in preparing direct mail solicitations for potential borrowers, working with advertising to sell the service to the public, and selling it to the branch managers themselves. With a few years experience, you may move up to product manager, and then Marketing Manager. Upper level bank marketing executives are well compensated, commanding $50,000 to $60,000 a year and more.

Finally, a banking background is good preparation for a good many careers outside of banking itself. Government agencies such as the Federal National Mortgage Association (Fannie Mae), the Federal Housing Administration (FHA) and the Veterans' Administration (VA) are always looking for experienced mortgage lenders. Your familiarity with housing loan regulations and procedures will make you very attractive to such institutions. Independent finance companies, like AVCO or Household Finance, also employ qualified former bank lenders. So do automobile companies, such as General Motors for their GMAC credit division.

Experience in customer service, of course, is transferrable to many other industries outside of banking. Law offices, for example, serve as solicitors for estates of deceased clients, and employ experienced former bank administrators familiar with state and federal regulations and taxes pertaining to escrow accounts. Credit companies, like American Express, will be very interested in your bank customer representative credentials as well. All in all, a banking background can be your ticket to career success in many related fields.

SPECIALTIES

At one time, a bank was a place to borrow money for a house and to store whatever you had left. Period. Like the 4% mortgage loan, those days are over. Today, banks are involved in every imaginable type of financial transaction, including (but not limited to) money market investing, brokerage services, credit cards, individual retirement and pension accounts, personal loans and business underwriting. This diversity has created the need for a high degree of specialization among banking professionals.

First and foremost is still mortgage lending. Over the years, the local, state and federal governments have managed to so complicate the simplest real estate transactions that it is virtually impossible to buy or sell a property without an army of assistants. Chief among these is the mortgage lender. To begin with, it quite literally takes years to become completely familiar with all of the different forms, rules and procedures involved in applying for any type of government guaranteed loan. Since over 50% of all mortgage loans fall into that category, you better believe that mortgage lenders have to keep current on all that. Indeed, applying for an FHA mortgage is a lot like the old comedy routine where a man orders a sandwich, and his waitress presses him endlessly for clarification. What kind of lunch meat? What kind of bread? Lettuce? Tomato? Mayonnaise or mustard? Fixed or variable rate? How large of a down payment? Private mortgage insurance required? There is even a requirement that the purchased home have a bathroom on the bedroom level to qualify for an FHA loan!

Aside from understanding the procedures, mortgage loan officers must become very knowledgable about the local real estate market. Since the collateral offered for a real estate loan is the property itself, banks want to be very sure that they are not lending more than a property is worth. Should they ultimately become the owners, they have to sell and get back the full amount. Since the most important factor in determining a property's worth is location, the mortgage lender must know local real estate values. In addition, the lender must look at the buyer's intended use of the property. Do zoning ordinances permit him to build the condo complex he has planned? Are there any title restrictions on the property itself? And is the venture likely to succeed, if the housing units will front an interstate highway? All of these things must be determined to properly evaluate the risk of any given loan.

Another area of specialization is brokerage services. Mentioned briefly earlier, the type of brokerage service usually offered by banks mostly involves quoting stock and bond prices and processing customer transactions. Very rarely do bank brokers offer investment advice. They are not required to be licensed brokers, nor do they receive commissions for selling particular stocks or bonds. Bank brokers are paid strictly on salary, usually between $18,000 and $26,000 (with a little experience.)

Most likely, you first will become familiar with your bank's brokerage services as a customer representative, where you may explain the service to depositors, open new accounts, etc. If you are interested in pursuing it as a specialty, you probably will start out on an order desk, processing customer buy and sell orders. Here you will learn about limit and market orders, bid and ask price spreads, splits and dividends, yields and P/E ratios. Once you are knowledgable enough to understand customer instructions, you will be assigned certain accounts, and will give quotations, take orders and place them with the listed exchange representatives.

Lastly, many banks now offer their customers specialized financial planning. For instance, if a customer wants to create an income trust for a favored charity, a bank financial planner will help determine how large an endowment is necessary to produce the desired income, how to structure the estate to get the most favorable tax treatment, etc. Similarly, a self-employed customer may wish to open a Keogh account for his retirement. The bank planner examines the individual's financial situation and offers plans best suited to the customer's needs.

Whatever specialty you choose to pursue, the time to begin preparing for your career in banking is now. Again, I want to emphasize that there is a great deal of opportunity in banking for non-degreed applicants, but you will need some basic skills, both from your education and experience.

--------- PREPARATION ---------

While in high school, you definitely should take as many business and math courses as possible. If your school offers economics and/or accounting, take them too. You need to be completely comfortable working with figures. Also, a good understanding of basic accounting practices will help a great deal. In concrete terms, you should be able to perform basic functions such as computing compound interest, comparing different rates of return, and determining the present value of future income.

In addition, it is vital that you become computer literate. It's a trendy term, but the importance of good computer skills cannot be overstated. A lot of your initial responsibilities, whether you start as a loan processor, bank teller or customer service representative, will involve computers. In banking today, all account information is computerized. To do even the simplest thing, like prepare a monthly statement or submit a loan application, requires data entry skills. No other single skill is more likely to land you that first banking job. Beyond that, you certainly will need to be comfortable with the bank's systems to continue in lending, brokerage services or what have you. Be smart. Learn the ins and outs of computers now. It's free. It's painless. And at this point, it's the best career investment you can make.

If you feel at all weak in math or accounting skills, I strongly advise you to get a tutor or take remedial courses. A good way to evaluate yourself, believe it or not, is to take the SAT (and you thought you were getting out of it). Although some of it deals with logarithms (which everyone was wrong about, you won't ever use them), a lot of the math section is devoted to that popular favorite, the word problem. Since your customers will speak to you in words, and you will answer in numbers, these are particularly good practice for banking work. In any case, scoring well on the math portion on your SAT's will be a good recommendation. A poor performance will identify weak areas where you need improvement.

There are also many ways to gain practical experience which will help you get that first bank job. In school, become involved in the financial end of organizations. Be the class treasurer, or treasurer for a club.. This will familiarize you with accounting procedures like credits and debits, general ledger balancing and running balances. Also, your participation in these groups will demonstrate fiscal responsibility and integrity.

Another good way to get experience is to volunteer as business manager for a school group, like the yearbook or drama club. Here, in addition to working the numbers, you should get involved in some financial planning. Are funds needed to finance a special event? How much and when? How can they be raised? Developing these types of business plans will be good experience for future banking responsibilities.

Outside of school, there are a lot of ways to get practical experience in banking skills. Volunteer to work as treasurer for a local civic group, such as a volunteer fire association. Take responsibility for the financial aspects of special events like pancake breakfasts, bingo nights or carnivals. Help with mailings to drum up new members. Not only is this good experience, it shows you to be exactly the type of solid citizen banks value and hire.

The important thing to keep in mind is that you have a lot to offer a potential banking employer. Do not make the mistake of selling yourself short. Many people have an image of banking as a profession for loftier individuals than you and I. This is just not true.

Certainly, to be successful in banking requires ambition, some basic skills, a little luck and a willingness to work hard, but this is true of any career. The fact that you do not have a college degree is of very minor importance in banking, especially at the entry level. And since the hardest step up any ladder is the first one, once you get a leg up, you should let nothing stop you.

3

Commercial Art

If it is true that a picture tells a thousand words, then commercial artists are the most widely read professionals in the world. While few hopefuls succeed in the "fine arts," commercial artists belong to that blessed minority of people who get paid for doing what they love. Commercial art is literally all around us, from highway billboards to newspaper circulars, television commercials to milk cartons. If you have an interest in and talent for drawing, but always thought you would have to learn to type to make a living, I have great news — you can make a wonderful living as a commercial artist!

That's the good news. The bad news is that lots of other people are already in on the secret. There is intense competition for commercial art jobs, especially in advertising agencies. A single opening has been known to attract hundreds of applicants. With those odds, even very promising people can be passed over. Fortunately, ad agencies are not the only place to do art work, and you may want to consider starting out in one of the other industries that employ artists. There are many.

Careers in commercial art are as varied as they are exciting, and every one of them offers tremendous opportunity for non-degreed candidates. Like other professions where the strongest emphasis is placed on results, you will find that your ability and drive weigh far more heavily in your favor than a sheepskin might. Successful non-degreed artists work in advertising, printing, packaging, illustration and architecture, to name some areas. Let's look at them in more detail.

——————— PEOPLE IN COMMERCIAL ART ———————

By far the most common arena in which commercial art careers are fulfilled is advertising. There are opportunities for artists of all kinds to develop their skills and advance their careers in both agencies and corporate advertising departments. Imagine a television commercial without art! Annoying as we may find them now, they are for the most part visually pleasing, thanks to the artists. They are involved in the design of all types of ads, including tv commercials, newspaper and magazine advertisements, direct-mail pieces, and highway billboards. Commercial artists contribute to all phases of art production, from mechanical drawing and paste up/layout to set design and prop selection. In ad agencies, artists work closely with ad writers and clients to produce a finished ad that projects exactly the right product image.

In corporations, commercial artists perform many of the same functions and then some. Many companies have their own in-house advertising departments, usually in addition to one or more hired agencies. In a corporation, an artist may be involved in print ad production, but will also be more heavily involved in designing illustrated brochures for new product releases, artwork for company newsletters and annual reports, as well as product packaging.

Packaging in particular is an area often overlooked by aspiring commercial artists, and that is unfortunate, because packaging offers a lot of career opportunity. Also, there is somewhat less competition for packaging design positions than for agency art jobs.

Publishing people learned long ago that while it may be true you cannot judge a book by its cover, the right cover can make you buy it. That is where packaging artists come in. Almost every product sold today is packaged in some way. The principal purpose is to attract consumers. Of course the box keeps all the Cheerios together, but why is it a bright yellow? Why is there a picture of a bowl of the stuff on the box? Why indeed is it in a box at all, rather than a plastic bag or a glass jar? The answer is that people like it that way. They must, seeing how Cheerios is the most popular cereal in America.

The job of the packaging artist, then, is to display the product most attractively to the customer. This includes designing the package itself, as well as the labels, pictures, etc. The artist will produce the camera ready artwork, and may do the actual photography as well. In a very real sense, this all contributes to the product's (and therefore the company's) bottom line. Not all packaging artists work for manufacturers, though. Ad agencies often offer this service to their clients, as do independent packaging houses, and many packaging artists work as free-lancers. In any event, do not overlook packaging design as a foot in the door to commercial art. You just may like it so much you make it your specialty.

Another area of opportunity for commercial artists is illustration, particularly technical illustration. Like packaging, this is a good place to start, and it offers good career potential in its own right. Technical illustrators work mostly for manufacturers, but they also are hired by publishing houses, printers and police departments. Primarily, they are responsible for illustrating a particular product to scale, often from several different perspectives.

In publishing, illustrators depict what is being described in text, like those little drawings of bacteria in the encyclopedia. Also, trade journals and magazines employ commercial artists to illustrate the articles they print. For example, doctors who submit articles to the Journal of the American Medical Association rarely include snapshots of their new cataract removal technique. The journal's artists work with the writers to understand systems and procedures, and produce illustrative photographs or drawings. Many illustrators work on a free-lance basis, developing specialties and becoming known and recommended in a particular field.

Finally, you may choose to begin your commercial art career in printing. For years now, people have been predicting the demise of printing as we know it. Computer graphics, the wave of the future, were going to make conventional printing as out-dated as wolf bane and spats. Well, here we are in the mid-1980's, and printing is still going strong. And it will continue to prosper for the foreseeable future, simply because computers will never replace artists.

Printing artists can work for newspapers or magazines, book publishers, ad agencies or printing houses. They are responsible for everything from typesetting to custom plate design and lithographic reproductions. Many smaller companies do not have advertising departments or agencies to design their product bulletins, catalogs, etc. They rely on their printers for the artwork as well as the production of these important items. In publishing, printing artists set type as well as design and produce plates for illustrations and photographs. All in all, printing is not only excellent experience for any other commercial art career you may decide on, it offers exciting careers all its own.

We have seen that opportunities in commercial art are everywhere. While the field is highly competitive, there definitely is room for talent, particulary if you are flexible about where you begin. Of course, wherever you begin, you will be at the bottom. What are entry level art positions like? What do they pay? Let's look at that.

————————————— THE ENTRY LEVEL —————————————

Entry level jobs in commercial art are exercises in trial by fire. From the very beginning, you will have hands-on responsibility for things like ad paste-up and layout, typesetting, mechanical drawings and plate setting. A typical entry level job is layout artist.

As the term implies, layout artists lay out, on a board, the artwork for a particular ad. They then add any lettering, drawing, etc, and whatever else is necessary to make it "camera ready." Photographic prints are then taken, and sent for color separation and printing. Usually, you will spend two to three years in an agency or corporate ad layout position, gaining increased responsibility along with experience. You should be offered no less than $12,000 a year to start, more if the agency is in New York city (many large ones are).

Many large ad agencies have separate departments, really mini-companies, which produce video advertisements. Here you would start out selecting props and wardrobe, doing make up, working the lights, and generally assisting the art director with production of the commercials. After two or three years in production, you are ready to move into design work. Salaries in video are similar to those in print layout, unless you have training and/or experience in the technical end, i.e., shooting and editing film. These skills should bring your offer up to at least $18,000.

In illustration, you may start out with scale and perspective drawings of products. Alternatively, you may begin with instruction manuals. For example, a computer manufacturer may hire you to illustrate the execution of commands on a keyboard or loading of disks. If you have good photography skills, you may land a job with a magazine publisher or printer doing cover/text art. In any case, a full-time entry level illustration position should pay $12,000-$14,000. If you free lance, try to get at least $10 an hour.

As mentioned earlier, a good place to break into the field is packaging. Here you can start out with a manufacturer, an agency or an independent packaging house. Initially, you will be more involved with producing than designing the packages, doing camera art, lighting, etc. Expect to earn $13,000 to $15,000 your first year in packaging.

If you want to pursue a career where drawing skills are especially important, a good place to get experience is in drafting, or mechanical drawing. Drafters are employed by architectural firms, engineering job shops, mechanical design companies and other businesses. While drafting is not technically considered an art, it really is no different than preparing mechanical drawings for an ad campaign or illustrating a new car design. Furthermore, drafting is a great place to perfect your commercial skills, as you learn all about dimensions, scale, perspective and other vital elements of illustration, An entry level drafting position should pay $14,000 to $17,000 with a manufacturer or job shop, a bit less for an architectural firm.

If you have studied or worked in photographic art, you might look for an entry level position with a real estate firm, magazine or newspaper, photography studio or ad agency. Your skills in lighting, exposure, framing and developing could land you a photographic assistant's job at a studio or ad agency. In agency or studio work, you may at first be responsible mainly for setting up shoots, arranging and testing lighting, enlarging prints, etc. This is first rate experience for future commercial art positions like agency art director or publishing artist. Consider also work for real estate firms, who need free lancers to shoot spreads of listed properties. Small businesses, too, contract photographers to do artwork for product brochures, press releases, etc. It's hard to estimate what kind of income to expect from entry level photographic work, but it's safe to say it won't be much. The main value in this type of work is the experience and skill development it provides. A strong background in commercial photography, especially video production, is like money in the bank as you progress.

In all honesty, however, people do not go into commercial art for the money. Although it is entirely possible to make a very comfortable living at it, the real enjoyment, like so many creative professions, is in the work itself. Commercial art offers a unique and exciting environment in which to make a buck.

Advertising artists, for example, can become involved in an almost limitless variety of media. Print ads, outdoor advertising, and direct mail campaigns require skill in drawing, photography, design and layout. Television commercials call for lighting, set design, taping and editing ability. In packaging design, artists work with textures as well as visual arts. The work environment is fast paced, challenging, creative, rewarding and fun! It can also be frustrating, demanding and high pressure. It is never routine.

Careers in illustration have their own charms. To properly represent a product, technique or object, you must understand it intimately. Anatomical illustrators, for example, spend long hours studying the structures and relationships of skeleton and musculature. At what angle does the arm protrude from the shoulder when throwing a baseball? When the back arches, how are stomach muscles affected? How do they look? Only after these and many other questions have been answered does the illustrator lift his pencil.

Many illustrators work on a free-lance basis, which offers the ultimate degree of personal freedom. While you cannot really work only when and where you want (at least not if you want to eat), you will work on a great diversity of assignments, as well as have time to enjoy the money you make. Even if you work full-time for a corporation or publisher, you will have the satisfaction of creating something all your own, and learning a lot in the process.

Overall, careers in commercial art are exactly what the term implies — an exciting mix of business and creativity. From an image perspective, too, the commercial artist has the best of both worlds. Artists, while often admired, are generally thought of as just a little flaky, if not downright irresponsible. Business, on the other hand, has the reputation of being routine and confining. As a commercial artist, you can have a fine time drawing pictures and getting paid for it, and no one will say a word. What a career! And it gets better.

CAREER PATHS

Careers in commercial art fall roughly into two categories — the business and the technically oriented. Business careers include advertising art, whether for an agency or a corporation, packaging art and printing. The most common path is through advertising, so we will look at that first.

As I have described, advertising artists usually begin in paste up and layout. Expect to spend a good two to four years there, gaining hands-on experience "on the board." After that, you will move into a full artist position, with responsibility for given campaigns and/or products. Not only will you be involved with ad production, you will begin to have greater creative input, designing sets, selecting models and props, arranging displays, etc. You will work closely with the agencies or companies' writers, actually creating a complete product image. This can be a highly visible position, and top artists are recognized and rewarded. The ultimate reward is promotion to Art Director.

Agency Art Directors are powerful people. They may have direct creative responsibility for key accounts, but primarily they direct the efforts of the artists under them. The Art Director sets the tone for all of an agency's work. Experienced people in the business can easily identify an ad or commercial from a particular agency by its distinctive style. Of course, different clients and products require different types of campaigns, but there is almost always an underlying unity to an agency's work. That is the influence of the Art Director.

But the life of an Art Director is not completely charmed. Much of the day is taken up with administrative tasks. The Director has total responsibility for art personnel, including hiring, training, supervising and evaluating artists, as well as advising them on artistic points and lending a sympathetic ear. In addition, the Art Director must work within a budget, keeping records of and a close eye on costs. For all of this, there is more than personal satisfaction. Top agency Art Directors earn $60,000 or more in salary alone, depending on the size and location of the firm. On top of that, there is usually a performance bonus in the form of stock or cash.

Packaging careers are equally rewarding, artistically if not financially. Again, at the entry level, you will be responsible mainly for production in the way of lighting and setting up for product shoots, laying out the artwork, setting up labels, etc. Once you have a few years experience, with either a corporation or a packaging house, you will be given responsibility for creating completely new packages from scratch. You will select shapes and colors, decide on lettering, choose between photographs and illustration and design labels. It is very satisfying to take this type of job from start to finish, knowing that your efforts will have great impact on the product's success. Experienced packaging artists earn $40,000 a year and more full-time, though many work on a free-lance basis. There top people can command $25 an hour or more.

A third commercial art career path is in printing. Starting in typesetting, you will spend two to three years learning the ropes, actually working with the equipment, doing page set-up, cold type,etc. Once you are familiar enough with the printing process, you will get involved with plate design, color separation, material selection and copying. Experienced print artists can earn $30,000 or more, but the real opportunity lies in starting your own print shop.

Printing has always been predominantly a mom and pop type of industry. Except for a few franchised chains, who really do not do much artistic work anyway, print shops are small businesses where artists are owners and customers are neighbors. It seems there is always room for a good printing house. While magazine and book publishing provides steady work for the shop, there are relatively few publishers, and the majority of printers make their living from small businesses and individuals. For every wedding there are invitations to be made and stationery to be personalized. The firehouse needs posters to advertise the turkey dinner. And the real estate brokers need listing brochures printed every month or so. What you make as a printer is really up to you, but the fringe benefits of owning your own business should make anyone interested in this field seriously consider this avenue of commercial art.

There is also a lot of opportunity in illustration. Commercial artists work as illustrators in business, publishing and architecture, to name some areas. In a corporation, an illustrator will be responsible for a particular product. That means that he must know not only that product, but what similar products are on the market and who buys them. For example, an artist hired to illustrate the XYZ Co.'s new line of copiers does not simply sit down and draw them. He first examines the product. What does it do better than its competition? Perhaps it has more sorting trays or an easier-to-use paper feeding system. Those features will be highlighted and shown in detail on product bulletins and advertisements. Different drawings will be used to illustrate operating instructions, and still others to guide service technicians. Thus, the artwork itself is only the most visible part of the product illustrator's work.

In publishing, illustrators have a more elusive job — to capture the essense of a writer's meaning in pictures. Book publishers use illustrators for cover artwork, be it a photograph or drawing. For the text, artists illustrate both in the sense of showing what is being described and creating images to enrich the story. Thus, you may find yourself drawing rubber trees for Mr. Webster and birthday birds for Dr. Seuss. Either way, you can earn a good living, with experienced ilustrators earning $25,000 to $40,000 a year. Here, too, many people work free-lance, working for as much as $30 an hour.

A somewhat less free-spirited career path for commercial artists is mechanical and architectural drawing, or drafting. This type of drawing has its attractions, however, chief among them being steady work. Perhaps because it is the furthest from a fine art career, drafting is thought of as more of a "real job" than is illustration or photography. At the entry level, there is less competition for jobs than in other areas of commercial art, and the lack of an advanced degree is seldom a drawback. Drafters in business engineering departments are responsible for creating mechanical drawings, or blueprints, of products, often when they are only at the conceptual stage. Drawings are made to scale, a multiple or fraction of scale, side and top perspectives are given, cross sections are shown and details are enlarged. A single product may require several dozen blueprints (in triplicate), not to mention component parts drawings. This kind of work requires not only disciplined drawing, but strong math skills as well for calculating scales, ratios and dimensions.

You may choose to pursue a drafting career, in which case you will progress to designer and then Design/Drafting Supervisor. With five to eight years experience, a supervisor can earn $27,000 to 38,000 a year. Even if you move into another area of commercial art, a few years in drafting is top notch experience to have. It provides a certain discipline many artists never develop, as well as a steady cash flow. Some people work in drafting while pursuing advertising art or illustration on a free lance basis. In any case, drafting is an area of commercial art you should not overlook.

SPECIALTIES

Since the world of commercial art is so large and so varied, many artists develop specialties in particular areas. Once you have established a strong base of general experience, you may want to consider this. There are many to choose from, depending on where you are. In drafting, artists usually specialize in mechanical drawing of general product lines, like electronic equipment, automobiles or heavy machinery. A common specialty is architectural drafting.

Architecture design offices employ many drafters to prepare blueprints of many different types of structures. These artists are responsible for interpreting the designs of the architects, insuring that proper dimensions are maintained, allowing necessary clearances, and generally filling in the details of the design. Architectural drafters are the ones who turn ideas like "two story colonial with four bedrooms, two baths, and a skylight in the living room" into blueprints from which contractors can actually build something.

Similar to architectural drafting is civil engineering art. Though civil engineering is somewhat of a dying art, there always will be bridges to build and highways to lay out. Drafters in civil engineering prepare mechanical designs of very large structures, mostly in the public domain. Naturally, in drawing a new Hoover dam, drafters would work in teams, with each one responsible for only a portion of the total project. While jobs in the private sector may be shrinking, there is still opportunity in government, both military and civilian.

In illustration, artists specialize as well, usually by field. Because of the detailed knowledge required, illustrators concentrate on particular technical areas, such as anatomy, astronomy or veterinary medicine. Especially if you want to do free lance work at some point, you will be more marketable and more highly paid if you develop expertise in one or more related areas.

Advertising artists are almost forced to specialize from the beginning. Depending on the agency you sign with, you may work in print ad design or video, but rarely both. Video work usually requires advanced technical education, but there is definitely opportunity for talented and ambitious individuals who will put in the time and effort to learn, both formally and on the job. Many an assistant cameraperson has worked his way up to ad producer. Without the "book learning" up front, you will spend more time in lower level positions learning your trade. Though your career will advance more slowly than your more technically educated peers', the extra hands-on experience can only help in the long run, and you will catch up.

Most non-degreed agency artists, however, work in print ad design. Here too, your specialty will depend principally on the sort of firm you work for. Many agencies specialize themselves, doing primarily direct mail, outdoor advertising or color print advertisements, for example. While these are all distinctive types of advertising, the art skills required are very similar and highly transferable. You always will have a good employer pool, regardless of where you start out.

Some miscellaneous specialties to consider include sign painting, engraving, photographic reproduction, calligraphy, film animation and police drawing. Always be alert for special markets with special needs, and sell yourself accordingly. Use your creative talent to develop your career as well as your skills. Remember that the only limiting factor in reaching your career goals, whatever they may be, is your own imagination, and that opportunity knocks more often and loudly on the door of those who are prepared.

PREPARATION

As mentioned earlier, the single most important skill in commercial art is drawing. By that I mean the most basic executions — things like straight lines, angles of the correct degree and objects of the proper scale. Only a few unusual artists — Salvador Dali, for example — have prospered by drawing buildings with one wall higher than the others. Educationally, then, you should take as many drafting courses as possible.

Almost every high school has "shop"; take it — or them. I mean metal, print, wood and auto (why pay a mechanic?). If you are lucky enough to attend a school which offers a vocational-technical (VO-TECH) program, by all means sign up. These programs offer not only excellent drafting and printing courses, but job placement assistance as well.

Don't overlook the creative arts either. By high school you should be ready for relatively advanced training, and will be given the opportunity to learn about background and foreground, perspective, shading and color. Some schools offer photography courses as electives, and I encourage you to take those too. Learning how to make a picture look like what you see through your camera lens is a valuable career skill to acquire. Learn also to develop and print your own work. You will find that even more artistic control occurs after shooting the picture than before.

Finally, you should try to take relevant math courses like geometry and algebra. Learn about degrees of arc, parallel planes, tangents and ratios. These will be immensely helpful not only in drawing but photographic and video art careers as well. The basis of all good art, fine or commercial, is good technique. Maybe Picasso's subjects did not look real, but they looked like what he wanted them to look like. You too must develop this control, and to do it, you need the mathematical tools.

In addition to educating yourself in the arts, take advantage of the many opportunities for practical experience offered in school and elsewhere. Try to work on projects where you have a chance to experiment a little, as well as exercise what you learn in the classroom. Always be sure to keep records of completed work. This type of collection will serve as your beginning "portfolio," and you can start working on it now right in your own school.

Every high school has a yearbook, much as you might like to disown your picture in it later on. People are needed to layout the artwork, illustrate the covers and prepare the material for printing. And what about the "Things we'll never forget" page? Someone has to take those photos, and develop and print them, too. Consider also doing artwork for the class play program. I don't mean just illustrations, though they're great, but take cast pictures and shots of the dress rehearsals. Offer to do artwork for playbook sponsors (advertisers). If you have a school newspaper, submit editorial cartoons and do calligraghy.

Why not join the thespian society? Theatrical production is excellent experience for advertising art, and a lot of fun to boot. There are all kinds of jobs that go begging in theater. Someone has to work the lights, for example, and in that you will learn a lot about the effects of good and bad lighting, things like shadows and glare. Other jobs are make-up, wardrobe, set design and props. All of these are great ways to get your hands into making art, and that is crucial. Art, like love, must be experienced! Be sure to take pictures for the portfolio.

Projects in machine, metal and wood shop also can teach you a lot about the mechanics of good art. Here you will not only design and draw things, but build them too. There's nothing like a chair with one leg shorter than the others to show the importance of accuracy and attention to detail. Try out what you learn in the classroom on your own. Make a scale drawing of the gym, with maybe a detail of the scoreboard. Build a mock-up from your blueprints. Is it correct? The same can be done with metal shop projects. (Does your hamster have a proper cage?)

Outside of school there are also lots of good opportunities to develop your skills and portfolio. Volunteer your services in promotional artwork for civic groups and businesses. Better yet, enter contests. Here you not only work at your trade but get some publicity in the bargain. Of course, you have to win, and you will, once you have entered a few and learned how they work.

In art, like music, a lot of importance is attached to contests. Winning a major contest can "make" a career, or at least launch it. Such contests are sponsored by every imaginable group, from the milk marketers association to the local zoo. For example, the city of Philadelphia recently held a contest (open to amateurs only) for the best photographic images of the city and its people. The winning shots, with credits, were featured in a promotional brochure for tourists to Philadelphia. Businesses sponsor similar competitions for logo designs. Sometimes free lancers are invited to compete in advertising campaign contests. Even if you only compete in smaller local contests, the experience will be worthwhile. You might win something and you will be noticed.

Test your ability and mettle as much and as soon as possible. As Einstein said, genius is 2% inspiration and 98% perspiration. Talent alone will not carry you. Develop the discipline to do a job as it assigned; there may be no accounting for taste, but as a commercial artist, your work must do a job first and stun the critics second. Above all, don't listen to all those who tell you it can't be done. Most likely they had dreams once, too, but somewhere along the line they settled for less. They envy your determination to make a career of what you love. Show them all. Do it.

4

Data Processing

There has never been a better time than now to be starting a career in data processing. The exciting world of computers is constantly expanding and evolving. Technological improvements have created desktop models able to do the work of large mainframes that once took up entire rooms. And yet, all of the technological advances have created more — not less — opportunity in data processing.

Of course, data processing involves a lot more than "working with computers." Computers themselves cannot produce meaningful information, as the familiar term "garbage in, garbage out" implies. That is the job of the people in the data processing department.

Today's companies, even smaller ones, require such sophisticated and timely information about so many things it would be impossible for them to function without effective data processing departments. These departments, often called Management Information Systems (MIS) groups, are responsible for taking raw information from other departments (users), and producing reports, graphs, charts, etc. which present that information in a useful way. For example, let's say the Sales Manager comes to MIS with a job — to determine the effectiveness of a special promotion in selling a new product.

All of the necessary information to do this job is already in the computer, since such data as monthly sales are routinely entered into it. Why, then, can't the Sales Manager get the information himself? Quite simply, because he doesn't know how to ask the question in any form the computer can understand. A computer programmer, on the other hand, knows how to address the machine in the right language, ask the questions in the right order, and get meaningful answers.

It is not hard to imagine how much more complex "jobs" can become when we talk about large banks, insurance companies and government offices. In these areas computer professionals become highly specialized, and are sought after for their expertise in check processing, mortgage loan or actuarial applications.

————————PEOPLE IN DATA PROCESSING————————

Responsibilities in data processing generally are divided into two main categories: hardware and software. Hardware refers to the physical computer and related equipment (peripherals). People who work in computer hardware are involved in the design, manufacture, installation and repair of computers and peripherals. Except for positions in service (installation/maintenance), it is very difficult to work in hardware without a specialized college degree, namely, a BS in electrical engineering. For once, there is a reason for this. Computers are highly complex electronic devices which require very sophisticated knowledge to design and build. Happily, this is not always the case with software.

Software is just as complex in its own way, but it is an area in which on-the-job experience is required in addition to whatever education one may bring to the task. This is certainly an advantage for the skilled non-degreed applicant, because the employer will have to train anyway, so why should he a pay a premium for a degree when an intelligent non-degreed person can do the job as well or better.

The term software refers to the programs which make the computer work. These include the very basic "systems" programs which operate the machine, as well as "applications" programs which do specific jobs. People in software operate, program and analyze computer systems. There are also many areas related to computer software that present great opportunity to non-degreed applicants. These include software support, documentation, technical writing and user training.

Within both hardware and software are computer-related careers. Technically knowledgable people are in constant demand by manufacturers, distributors and service companies to perform such jobs as sales, marketing, product management, training and customer service. Again, these are fields in which experience, ability, people skills and a willingness to work hard and learn are valued more highly than a degree.

The world of data processing has recently experienced another major division worth noting, the one between micro and mainframe computers. The data processing departments we have been talking about in banks, insurance companies and other large organizations use multiple mainframe (large) computers to process the huge volume of information they require. The vast majority of these mainframes are manufactured by IBM, and run programs written in the computer language COBOL. Whatever other training and/or experience you may have is pretty much irrelevant to these large companies if you do not also know IBM COBOL. I mention this primarily as a warning. The majority of jobs in data processing are in big business-and big business uses IBM COBOL. Learn it.

On the other end of the spectrum are micro (small) computers. This is certainly the high technology growth field of the future. As small computers become more powerful, they are able to take the place of mini and even mainframe computers in many cases. Careers in microcomputers generally do not involve working in data processing departments, mainly because micros are used primarily in small companies, or even in the home. Also, a major selling point of the micro manufacturers is the "user-friendliness," or ease of operation, of their systems. A real estate broker who buys a microcomputer intends to run it himself, using pre-packaged software and the manual (and body english.)

Of course, someone has to write the software, prepare the manual and train the real estate broker, and these are all areas exploding with career opportunity for the non-degreed applicant. Software for micros is written by independent software houses, as well as computer manufacturers. There are literally thousands of software houses, all looking for skilled people to write the Ultimate General Ledger package. By far the greatest opportunity for those with people skills, however, is the area of support.

Most people who buy small computers are overwhelmed by them. Smart retailers have caught on to this, and are making a fortune selling "peace of mind"; in other words, training, service and support. Someone with a good understanding of micro operations and software is invaluable, both to the eager seller and the bewildered buyer.

Whether you choose to pursue a career in hardware or software, micros or mainframes, the hard truth is that you will not start at the top. The right entry level position, however, can go a long way toward getting you there.

——————— THE ENTRY LEVEL ———————

Entry level jobs in data processing are varied and relatively plentiful for both degreed and non-degreed applicants with the proper skills and experience. The important things to consider when choosing an entry level position are not so much starting salary but responsibilities and opportunities for technical challenge and career growth. Although it may be a comparatively easy field to crack, it is not likely you will go very far in DP without further training and education. Even degreed people in the field realize the importance of keeping up with the latest developments in computer technology, and are constantly learning through evening courses, self-study and industry training seminars.

——— ENTRY LEVEL JOBS IN MAINFRAMES ———

Careers in mainframes, especially for non-degreed entrants, begin in operations. Computer Operators are responsible for running jobs given to them by programmers. Since even large computers cannot keep all necessary information in working memory, a large part of the operator's job is loading the proper disks (or tapes on older systems) into the computer for particular applications. This type of work requires a good knowledge of Job Control Language (JCL), the computer language with which the operator edits screens and sequences jobs to be run. It also provides valuable hands-on experience with the computer itself, teaching the operator the commands and keystroke sequences required to do different functions. This experience is very useful as you progress into programming. In fact, a major complaint DP managers have about Computer Science grads is that they have very limited exposure to operations, and have little appreciation for what is involved.

The most important thing to look for in an entry level operations job is the right equipment, namely IBM. Since most companies (over 80%) use IBM mainframes, having IBM experience is like having type "O" blood. The minority of companies who use other manufacturers' machines, such as Burroughs, Honeywell or Univac, will accept you and train you to use their systems. However, very few IBM shops will consider training someone with Honeywell experience to use their IBM equipment. Do not limit opportunities by starting out on the wrong equipment. After all, as a non-degreed applicant, you are selling experience, and the wrong experience is worse than none, as it shows poor judgment in your career planning.

What can an entry level computer operator expect to earn? Unless you live in New York City or Southern California, where salaries are doubled to compensate for a cost of living three times the national average, you should be offered between $12,000 and $14,000 a year to start. You may possibly go as high as $16,000 at a large company, if you have part-time work experience or other related skills. Less than $11,000 is unacceptable.

—————————WORK ENVIRONMENT—————————

Large companies run their computers around the clock. Indeed, they must, considering the cost of their equipment and the backlog of jobs with which most DP departments are faced. Naturally, this means that someone must always be there to run the machines, and you probably will be expected to work shift work at first. Usually, shifts are divided into day (7:00 a.m. - 3:00 p.m.), evening (3:00 p.m. -11:00 p.m.) and night (11:00 p.m. - 7:00 a.m.). One advantage to this system is that experienced operators are constantly leaving night jobs for day ones elsewhere, so there are usually some night/evening openings for entry level applicants. Once you are experienced, you too can turn your nose up at night work.

Operators, of course, work in data processing departments, and the work environment is unique. MIS is by far the most egalitarian department in any company. There is very little importance attached to titles and degrees. What counts is getting the job done, and beginners are encouraged to make suggestions and try new approaches. Looking out into a computer room, it is often difficult to tell the tape librarians from the systems analysts, as both are likely to be cross-legged on the floor, drawing yellow lines across endless piles of printouts.

MIS departments are also the least formal departments in most companies. Even DP Managers wear ties for special occasions only, and this attitude trickles down to the computer "floor." This makes it easy to pick out the DP'ers in the lunchroom. Do not, however, abuse this laxity, or you will find yourself in front of a terminal for a long, long time.

All of this laid back, democratic philosophy should not deceive you into thinking data processing is an easy career. The MIS department is typically one of the most fast-paced in the company, with tremendous emphasis placed on the completed job. When deadlines approach, operators, programmers and managers alike work long hours to meet them. There is little room for non-performers. Conversely, talent is rewarded, usually sooner than later.

─────── ENTRY LEVEL JOBS IN MICROS ───────

The world of microcomputers is generally a little more difficult for the non-degreed beginner to break into, not necessarily because they are ignorant, but because they are years younger than their degreed counterparts. Most jobs in microcomputers involve dealing with the public, and many people fresh out of high school are simply not mature enough to inspire confidence in some poor soul about to plunk down thousands of dollars for a box with blinking lights. He wants Ozzie Nelson, not Richie Cunningham. There are several ways to get around this common objection.

First, there are jobs in which you can gain computer experience without public contact. Primarily, these involve documenting and writing user manuals for microcomputers and their software. Most of these jobs are with computer or software manufacturers. Here it is sometimes better to look for the lesser known companies. Everybody writes programs for Apple and IBM micros, because that is what most people buy. Most, but not all. All of the other micro-manufacturers, who want to be the next Apple Computer, realize that to sell their equipment, they need to make the popular programs run on their systems, too. Likewise, software manufacturers want their programs to be as universal as possible, and need people to tailor their programs to run on Zenith and Compaq micros. Someone familiar with the Zenith system could tailor a word processing program to run on that computer, document it, and write the user manual.

Another way to break into a microcomputer career is through retail sales. Although it may seem a bit backwards, retailers and distributors are always more interested in your ability to close a sale than grow a beard. Once you have proven your expertise and maturity behind the counter, you are more likely to be considered for a customer service or training position.

What can you expect to earn as an entry level microcomputer documenter? The range is generally $14,000 to $16,000 a year. Anything less than $12,000 for a full-time position is too low to consider. In retail sales, you probably will work on a salary plus commission. The total package, without unrealistic sales expectations, should be between $15,000 and $18,000 a year.

WORK ENVIRONMENT

Positions in documentation and manual writing allow great independence and often flexible work schedules. Of course, when there are product release deadlines to be met, that flexibility takes the form of stretching the work day. Generally, however, documentation is not a high pressure position.

Many of the responsibilities in documentation seem repetitive and routine, and they often are. This is exactly what you want in your first position. Nothing teaches a skill like practice, practice, practice. The fact that you have run the same program over 500 times, trying to eliminate the necessity of endlessly swapping disks, means that you know that program type and that system very well indeed. Writing user manuals forces you to translate the documentation into clear and easily understandable instruction sets, which is precisely what you will do later with "users" (customers) when you move into customer service or training.

Since most microcomputer careers, starting in either sales or software, usually involve a lot of public contact, a high premium is placed on professionalism in dress and conduct. Remember that your youth is a liability initially, and you would be well advised to develop a mature business demeanor.

CAREER PATHS

Whether you choose to work in micros or mainframes, your career possibilities will follow two general paths. Although virtually everyone, degreed or no, begins in a hands-on computer position, you do not have to stay there.

Many people love the technical challenge today's computers provide, and they progress through higher and higher levels within programming and analysis. Others elect to use their technical backgrounds as stepping stones to more business-oriented positions within their companies.

OPERATIONS AND PROGRAMMING

As stated earlier, many people begin their computer careers as operators. Although most then move into programming, some do remain in operations, advancing into positions of greater responsibility in that area. The usual progression is from operator to Lead Operator/-Shift Supervisor, then Assistant Director, and finally Director of

Operations. A Director of Computer Operations usually will have 8-10 years experience in the field, and may earn up to $50,000 a year.

A career in operations requires both an in-depth knowledge of computers and their peripherals, and the entire data processing system as a whole. Operations Managers are responsible for maintaining the smooth functioning of the Computer Room. This is no small task, and it involves not only the equipment, but hiring, training and supervising all operations personnel, interfacing with vendor sales and service people, and representing Operations' needs to the rest of the company. With computers, there is always a crisis, and the "man of the hour" usually is the Operations Director.

For those who choose to move into programming, there also are exciting careers to pursue. As a beginning programmer, you will be responsible for writing code, that is, debugging or actually writing programs which a more senior programmer or perhaps an analyst has "speced out" (developed). Once you have mastered this (1-2 years), you may become a programmer/analyst, and then a systems analyst. These positions allow much greater interaction with others, both in the department and in user groups. P/A's and S/A's take a job from beginning to end, flow-charting the logic, writing complex parts of the program, determining how many programmers should take how long to code it, and assigning and supervising those tasks-as well as debugging and rewriting. This middle position of P/A or S/A is invaluable experience for the upwardly mobile DP'er, as it allows an opportunity to "see the whole picture", while at the same time keeping your hands-on technical skills sharp. It will also be your first taste of management. If it tastes good, after 4-6 years as a P/A or S/A, you may move into Project Management, then Assistant Programming Supervisor, Manager of Systems and Programming, and finally, MIS Director.

The road to MIS Director is a long one, requiring perhaps 12-15 years experience at the least. It can be a rewarding position financially, paying in the range of $45,000-$70,000 a year. It is also a job with great responsiblilty.

The MIS Director is responsible for the entire Data Processing department, including the computers and related equipment, their installation and operation, programming and support. All positions in data processing report to the Director, though he or she does not normally directly supervise any but the highest level managers. In many companies, the DP department functions as an outside contractor, to which users come with their jobs. The MIS Director, or the staff, meet with users, determine the feasibility and costs of jobs requested, and sequence them by priority. Obviously, this does not lead to tremendous popularity, as there are always more jobs (all marked "Super Hot") to be run than machine time to do them. But the MIS Director interfaces with others in the company in more ways than one.

As the top man in a vital department, the MIS Director represents Data Processing and its interests in upper management meetings. Just as the Director of Finance may argue against a proposed equipment purchase, so the MIS Director will lobby for it on the basis of increased efficiency, less labor intensive operation, or greater speed of processing. To make his or her case effectively, the Director must be able to explain technical concerns to non-technical peers in other areas of the company. This is why the Director must be as much a teacher and politician as a technician, and to get to the top in DP requires excellent communication skills.

We have so far been discussing only one side of programming, called Applications. There is another type of programming, with its own demands and career possibilities, and that is Systems.

Systems Programmers are the technoid's technoids, the gurus of software. While those in Applications write programs to run jobs, systems people write programs that run the computer. Applications people use computer languages like COBOL and FORTRAN, designed to do certain tasks most efficiently. Systems programmers write in machine language, assemblers and compilers.

The "systems" in systems programming refers to the operating system of the computer. This is the master program on top of which applications are run. Operating systems are extremely complex beasts, and it would be the study of many li es to fully understand them. Nonetheless, systems programmers try to do just that, so they can fix what goes wrong and maximize the computer's output. A large part of the systems person's job is called capacity planning. Quite literally, it must be determined how much will fit in the computer for how long. As computer time is very expensive, the more jobs that can be done at once, the better. Extracting the most from a computer involves streamlining its operating system to handle data more efficiently.

Typically, a systems programmer will spend 8-10 years in an intense hands-on position before he is considered for management. Even then, the temperament required of good systems people is such that many prefer to remain in "techie-land," specializing in one or another arcane yet vital division of systems. Someone must be in charge, however, and ambitious systems programmers can advance to Team Leader, Assistant Systems Programming Manager and finally Systems Programming Manager. This position usually reports directly to the S&P Manager, and involves mainly hiring, training and supervising more junior personnel in the group.

There is little opportunity for interdepartmental exchanges in systems. There are, however, many advantages to the systems life. For one, good systems programmers are very well compensated, earning up to $50,000 a year. There may be flexible work schedules, and companies are eager to keep their systems people technically sharp, so there is a lot of gratis training provided via seminars and conferences. Also, systems people are seldom bothered with the political in-fighting that can plague other careers in data processing. Finally, there is a great deal of respect — almost reverence — accorded The Systems Programmers. They understand The Machine. They leap tall buildings in a single bound. They eat dinner at 10:00 a.m. And they are happy.

SUPPORT

Support refers to the myriad of DP related careers you may wish to pursue once you have established your technical credentials. In the mainframe area, most support positions are with manufacturers and distributors of computer equipment and software services. People with strong technical skills are in demand for jobs such as Product Manager, Sales Executive, Marketing Representative, Customer Service Manager and Training Coordinator. These positions require excellent communication skills, customer concern, business savvy and the ability to maintain your composure at all times.

DP related careers in industry can be quite lucrative. Salaries range from $24,000 a year for a distributor Customer Service Manager to $60,000 and up for Marketing Managers in software services firms. There is some truth to the DP Managers' lament that the salesmen who call on them drive better cars, as computer industry sales positions can pay above $75,000 with commissions.

In the microcomputer area, the majority of career opportunities are in this field of support. The focus, however, shifts from manufacturers to retailers, where technically proficient people are needed to assist customers with equipment and software selection and to provide training.

It is hard to identify a typical microcomputer career path. The industry is still very young, and adventurous souls are continuing to explore where their talents can take them. We can, however, look at some areas of opportunity.

The field of microcomputing is bursting with entreprenurial spirit. Who has not heard the story of the two college drop-outs who started Apple Computer (now a half billion dollar company)? While clearly not everyone can enjoy that degree of success, nonetheless your own business in microcomputers can be a very real goal. Once you have gained the necessary technical and business experience, your best bet may be to get into a franchise retail outlet such as Computerland or Entré Computer Stores. Although the cost of entry can be high ($40,000-$60,000), you can borrow or find partners. If you are successful, your investment will be repaid many times over.

An even more popular alternative for the free-spirited micro careerist is consulting. As microcomputers and their software become more powerful, their applications in small to medium sized businesses are expanding rapidly. Almost everyone realizes that they should probably "go on the computer." Exactly what that involves, and how to do it, remains a mystery, the solution to which is being provided increasingly by independent small business system consultants.

Such consultants take responsibility for the entire computerization process, starting with an in-depth analysis of the client's business and systems. He or she then recommends appropriate equipment and software to do the jobs required, installs the system, customizes software packages where necessary, trains the client's personnel in the use of the computer, and supervises the transition from manual to parallel to automated systems. Clearly this all requires more than technical expertise. Small business computer consultants must keep on top of new products, have a good understanding of general business practices and be able to market their services. And they are well paid for those services. Free lance consultants charge from $25 to $150 an hour, and get it. Although they are not on assignment 52 weeks a year, and there are expenses involved, consulting can provide a good living, and a satisfying life.

SPECIALTIES

Data processing is a career in which it is almost impossible to avoid specialization. Today's computer systems are so complex and so large that one simply cannot master them in their entirety, nor do employers want you to do so. In fact, generalist programmers (derogatorily called "plain vanillas") do not command much in today's market. Far more sought after are specialists in such areas as communications, data base technology and special applications.

The career path presented earlier for applications programmers runs in more of a straight line than most actual careers will do. While the general direction is correct, most application programmers take detours through various specialties. This specialization can take two forms: by technology and by industry.

Programmers who choose to develop special skill in a particular technology will find themselves in great demand. There is a shortage of qualified people in communications and database systems, especially in what are called "on-line" applications, and this will continue for a while. A DB or CICS (communications) P/A can expect to earn from $26,000 to $35,000 a year, while a plain COBOL programmer with equal years experience will get only $22,000 to $28,000. What's more, the "vanillas" have considerably less job mobility.

Many DP'ers specialize in particular applications, such as Consumer Loan, Life Insurance or Work In Process. Although this tends to limit the pool of potential employers down the road (banks want banking programmers), there usually is enough opportunity within large industries to maintain plenty of career options. Furthermore, this is the more common road to upper management. While Data Base Administrators can and do become MIS Directors, it is more likely that such a position will be filled by someone who has worked his or her way up a more business oriented ladder, through Project Leadership and Assistant Management in Property/Casualty Systems, for example.

Like mainframes, the microcomputer field has its specialties, too. These are generally by industry. Small business consultants, for example, find niches for their services in areas such as group medical practice, real estate or accounting partnerships. There is little danger that specialization will limit your marketability, as there are literally hundreds of small businesses in every field within 200 miles of your home. The benefits are better understanding of client operations and needs, and word of mouth advertising (doctors hang out with other doctors).

PREPARATION

Data Processing is a career for which it is quite possible to prepare on your own, both educationally and in the hands-on manner. Virtually every high school in the country today has a computer (usually micros) and computer courses available to students. Indeed, many require such courses. In addition to these, it is strongly recommended that you take as many math courses as possible, and a class in Logic/Math Theory, if offered.

A great many excellent books are available for self study as well. Look for those that include exercises with general flow charts and logic, and require you to complete the programs. Hand in hand with this type of self instruction must go actual experience on a computer.

Try to become familiar with as many systems (and languages) as possible. Consider not only your school's equipment, but also the public library, personal computers of friends and/or relatives, and computers in companies where your parents/brothers/sisters work.

Although most systems to which you can gain access will be small, the important thing is to get the hands-on experience of working with *a* computer. Operating systems and languages vary from micros to mainframes, but on a very basic level, programming is programming. Jobs must be speced, flow-charted, written, debugged, rewritten, fine-tuned and run. At the entry level, your experience in these things will be more valuable than an intimate knowledge of any one system.

There are also a great many technical schools which offer certificate programs in computer operations and programming. Most offer part-time day/evening courses, and you should be able to complete a good program in 6-18 months. Look for those schools with the most modern equipment, and instructors who also work in the industry. Not only will their teaching be more relevant to the job world, but they will also be excellent references for you later on. Such instructors have a lot of valuable contacts, and may even have a job for you themselves. The cost of computer certificate programs varies greatly. However, a good school should cost no more than $1200 for six months of full-time instruction.

In addition to a good computer education, you will need some work experience in the field. The problem is that there are very few people willing to hire a completely unproven individual to "play" with something as important as their computer systems. The solution to this dilemna is volunteerism. The number of people and organizations interested in your services multiplies dramatically when you do not ask to be paid. This type of "give-away" work, either in high school or after graduation (when you are living at home and perhaps can afford no income for a few months), is probably the greatest career investment you can make.

The list of organizations to which you should "apply" is almost endless. It should definitely include the Red Cross, the League of Women Voters, The Elks, The Free Library, the Chamber of Commerce, the Zoological Society, the Clean Air Council and the Legal Aid Society. Every one of these groups in your town has a computer, and probably could use some expert help in using it. Keep printouts of all programs you write, and be sure to get letters of reference from someone high up in the organization.

Should a paying position open up, you will be the first considered (grants are given out every day). Even if no openings develop, this type of work is not only valuable experience, it exposes you to important contacts in the world of business you hope soon to enter. More than a few Chamber of Commerce members are also bank Vice Presidents. Who better to ask about job openings at Home Savings and Loan?

Another way to get experience is through contract work. Very often, non-profit organizations and government agencies have specific jobs that need to be done, but either they do not have the funds or enough work long-term to justify hiring a permanent employee. Such jobs are put out to independent contractors, who bid a fixed amount to complete the work. Naturally, your inexperience will dictate pricing your services quite low. At first, you may not see much, if any, profit from your efforts. This is not only because you aren't charging much, but in the beginning, it will be hard for you to estimate how long different jobs will take. Your $1100 bid may win you four months of work. Nonetheless, it is excellent experience, from which you will learn much, make contacts and get references.

As you will no doubt discover, getting that first job in DP is not easy, and it is small comfort to note that college graduates face the same difficulties. However, with the right preparation, clear goals and a lot of determination, you can be confident of success.

5

Fashion Merchandising

More than any other single influence, fashion creates the image of an era. Every generation has its "look." Indeed, nothing so dates photographs as the clothes people wore. Who has not looked at their parents' wedding pictures and exclaimed "Look at those shoes!" It's fun to match styles with periods, bringing to mind the flapper of the twenties, the zoot suits of the forties, bobby socks of the fifties and bell bottoms of the sixties. Even those of us who claim to disdain fashion are more conscious of it than we realize, and are instantly aware when something doesn't fit in. Wouldn't you notice someone in a tie-dyed shirt?

While many people think of fashion as something directed primarily at women, the market for men's fashions is tremendous, and is growing rapidly. Especially today, men are genuinely concerned with their images, and strive to "dress for success." Children's fashions is another big area, and it too is getting bigger. Merchandising all of these fashions is big business. Opportunities exist for non-degreed candidates in all areas of merchandising, from design and manufacturing to sales and retailing. Fashion careers are diverse and exciting, and include design, illustration, sales, merchandise display, and buying. Let's look at some of these jobs in more detail.

PEOPLE IN FASHION

Careers in fashion merchandising fall into two areas — manufacturing and retailing, with manufacturers' representatives bridging the gap. When people think of the glamour and glitter of fashion, they are thinking of manufacturing. The design houses of Christian Dior and Gucci are world renowned. Most fashion, however, is more down-to-earth in nature, and while the big names may set trends, few

few people actually buy "designer" clothing. Smaller houses and manufacturers may buy licenses to use certain designs, but more often they employ their own designers, who translate the season's "look" into clothing than can be worn to work, at a more or less reasonable cost. There is a lot of opportunity in this type of design for talented people, degreed or not.

Jobs in manufacturing include not only design but fashion illustration, sales and trade show display and coordination. Though not technically employed by manufacturers, agents (or representatives) work for clothing makers, selling their lines to department and specialty stores, as well as directly to the public. People are employed in manufacturers' showrooms to display merchandise and assist store buyers. This end of the business can be fascinating and fun; however, most fashion career opportunities are in retailing.

By far the most common jobs in fashion merchandising are retail sales. Virtually all retail careers begin "on the floor," for good reason. As glamorous as it may seem, fashion merchandising is a business like any other. To make money, a store must move product, and at the front line of that effort are the salespeople. The longer an item sits on the rack, the less profit is made when (and if) it is eventually sold. Too many markdowns too soon are a direct result of poor sales performance (and merchandise selection), and cut deeply into the bottom line.

Retail sales involves a lot more than working a cash register, and failure to recognize this is, I think, a big factor in the problems retailers are having with discount chains. Quite simply, salespeople must sell, and that means knowing the products, assisting customers with selection, keeping the display area neat and attractive, picking up on what moves and what doesn't, and passing this information on to buyers. In addition to jobs on the sales floor, retailers have sales managers who are responsible for their departments, stores, and eventually, entire chains. In these positions, sales executives work closely with buyers, deciding what to bring in each season. Decisions are based not only what will sell, but also how well a product fits in with the stores' image and other lines, and how much money can be made. Unless a store like The Gap plans to invest in an entire line of business attire, there is little point in buying paisley ties, trendy or no. Similarly, designer undies may sell like hotcakes, but if there is little profit in them, what's the point.

Another important job in retail merchandising is display. Any salesperson who has to tell you some drapey looking thing "looks great on" is working in a poorly displayed department. The purpose of displaying items attractively is to sell them, and this means not only putting together outfits and accessorizing, but making sure customers can get to the merchandise! There's nothing more frustrating than wading through aisles jammed with junk to examine forty-four pairs of pants crammed onto a rack meant for twenty, only to find that they're all size 38's. There is no excuse for this lack of consideration for customers, and it certainly isn't going to sell those pants.

People who work in display try to lay out their departments with like items grouped together so shoppers can find what they are looking for, compare styles and prices, etc. Mannequins and wall displays are designed to give shoppers some ideas about dressing items up or down. The same shirt can have three different looks when paired with first a sportcoat, then a sweater and finally a tie. The goal is to sell some additional items the customer initially may not have wanted, or thought he wanted.

As important to profitability as sales and display is inventory control. People who work in inventory, or stocking, determine the when and how much of merchandising. Is it better to have enough unusual sizes in stock to never miss a sale, or should you stock mainly common sizes and sell the odd ones only until they run out? If the store expects to sell 200 pairs of leather pumps, should they all be brought in (and thus paid for) at the start of the season? Could you schedule shipments instead? And what mix of colors is best? How a stock manager's heart sinks to hear, "I really wanted them in red," especially when he is sitting on twenty-five pairs of navy.

Finally, a lot of a store's success rests with its buyers. These are thought of as the glamour positions in fashion retailing, and to a degree, they are. Store buyers travel the world seeking the hottest looks, visiting the big design houses, attending fashion shows and negotiating purchases. They also spend countless hours bargain shopping in sweaty garment warehouses, agonizing over skirt lengths and taking a lot of heat when padded shoulders go "out" a week after the big suit shipment arrives. To avoid this, buyers spend a lot of time studying fashion trends. Much good may it do them! Last year's sales are about as accurate a predictor of this year's demand as star watching. Often a buyer does best to bring in the best of several different styles, selecting for quality more than fashion. He'll get lucky with something, and then he won't be able to keep it on the racks. It's a tough job, and it is far from over when styles have at long last been selected.

Buying anything means negotiating, and fashion buyers are notorious hagglers. The retail market is highly competitive. Customers want the best, but at the best price. To sell in volume and at healthy profit margins, buyers must pay as little as possible at the showrooms. Fortunately for them, clothing manufacturing is equally competitive, and sellers are under pressure to negotiate. If they don't, someone else will. The goal is to bring in just enough of the right merchandise to sell at full price. A visit to your local Sears will show how difficult a job that is.

Whether you choose to work in sales or stock, manufacturing or retailing, you must start at the bottom and work your way up. If it is any consolation, even people with degrees from prestigious fashion schools will start out where you probably will — "on the floor."

THE ENTRY LEVEL

Far and away the most common entry level job in fashion merchandising is retail sales. You can treat it as a job with a paycheck, or you can take the opportunity to learn as much as possible, do above and beyond what is required and smile while you do it. Believe me, if you choose the latter, you will be noticed instantly, and eventually rewarded for your efforts. In truth, there is a lot to learn from retail sales which will be of great value later on in sales management, display or buying. First and foremost is the chance to deal with that all-important animal, the customer.

Sadly, the only interaction most salespeople today have with their customers is ringing up purchases. It wasn't always so, and it shouldn't be now. Once upon a time, retail stores had floor managers who supervised the clerks. Clerks were expected to greet customers when they arrived, show them how the department was laid out, help them put together outfits, answer questions about merchandise, wait outside dressing rooms to exchange items for size if necessary and bring in one of the store tailors once a selection was made. Some of this still goes on in finer stores (mostly men's, for some reason), but in general, retail salespeople today are indifferent at best. I have even had some surly ones. You can be different.

Keep in mind that your primary responsibility is selling, and that means knowing your products. Examine items as they come in. What makes one white blouse different from another? Why is one $30 and the other $70? Learn about different materials and their care, so that you can answer customer questions. Experiment putting together outfits; this will give you some ideas for selling additional items when a customer tries on a pair of pants. Keep abreast of your stock situation. Are there more size 8's in the back? Bring them out when the racks are low. Many customers assume that only what's displayed is available, and you will lose sales if your racks and shelves are lean.

Being a good salesperson also means showing a genuine interest in your customers. If a shopper is looking for a navy jacket, walk around with them collecting several possibilities to be tried on. Suggest coordinating tops. Don't forget accessories, either. A couple of belts or hats can add up to some nice business. Most of all, be available. Run errands from the dressing rooms to get other sizes and colors. If what the customer wants is not available, find out if you are expecting any more of that item soon. Check for it with other stores in your chain.. Not only will your customers remember you, your efforts (and strong sales) will impress the right people higher up.

At first, you will see little financial reward. Most retail sales positions pay minimum wage or only slightly above. If you work in a smaller specialty shop or finer department store, you may be paid commission on your sales. Even then, you will not be in the lap of luxury. Expect to make about $10,000-$15,000 a year full-time. You should get generous discounts on store merchandise, and press continually to be considered for higher positions as they open up.

Another possible, though less common entry level job is inventory clerk/stock checker. This is an excellent place to learn about the product, what moves and what doesn't and when. Initially, you will be responsible for checking shipments as they come in, verifying packing slips against merchandise received, inspecting for damage, unpacking and putting items away in the back rooms, etc. You will also monitor display racks, replacing merchandise as it is sold. Most importantly, you will keep track of how much of what merchandise is sold so that the Inventory Control Manager can reorder if necessary, exchange slow moving items for credit and properly schedule shipments of new merchandise. Starting out in the stockroom gives you a first-hand look at the business end of the operation. It may be high fashion to the customer, but in the stock room, those Calvin Klein shirts might as well be bananas. There, the issues are not hem lengths but what size, when, how many and how much. It isn't called merchandising for nothing.

As an entry level stock person, you should earn between $11,000 and $13,000 to start. After 2-3 years of increasing responsibility, your experience might command $16,000. Beyond that, you will have to move into inventory management to advance financially.

Finally, you might begin your merchandising career in the front office as an expeditor. Expediting is a thankless job in any industry. It seems to be a sort of trial by fire for future buyers, and it must work, because buyers, especially fashion buyers, can be real tough cookies. In a perfect world, there would be no need for expeditors. Orders would be processed accurately and promptly, merchandise would be shipped on time (to the right address), items received would match items ordered in type and quantity, nothing would be damaged and no one would get parking tickets. Alas for utopia.

In reality, purchasing departments are in a perpetual state of emergency. The spring coat manufacturer is being struck by the truckers and cannot ship your order until summer. You receive the swimsuit order on time, only to discover that they are all size 4's. The stock room calls to say that they are receiving a shipment of 2400 pajama tops with no bottoms. All of these snafus fall squarely on the shoulders of the expeditor, whose job it is to trace lost orders, process returns for incorrect or damaged merchandise, cajole suppliers into turning orders around overnight and locating 2400 pajama bottoms in a hurry. After 2-3 years of this, you will be ready for either a purchasing career or a jacket with no arms.

One consolation is that expeditors are generally on a higher pay scale than salespeople or stock clerks from the beginning. Entry level expediting positions pay between $12,000 and $15,000 a year to start. In addition to expediting, you probably will need some experience on the floor before you become a store buyer, where salaries are nice indeed.

Like many of the careers in this book, while fashion merchandising can be lucrative, an equally important career dividend is job satisfaction. A career in fashion can be exciting, glamorous, hectic, frustrating, fast-paced, exhausting and fun! The work environment truly is unique. Business decisions involving millions of dollars are based on something as ephemeral as fashion trends. Every new season is a roll of the dice, with one heck of a lot riding on the toss. People in fashion merchandising are thus inherently risk takers, willing to take big chances for big rewards. Management styles are aggressive, to put it mildly. Intense pressure exists to produce or perish.

Fashion people also have a certain flair. Perhaps they are attracted to the industry for the opportunity to express their own sense of style, or maybe they develop that sense because they work with fashion. In either case, lifestyles tend to be unconventional. Fashion merchandising is a very cyclical business. Seasons come and go, and so do peak and slow periods. Fashion is also an international business, with fabric from India woven into Spanish style vests sold in Italian designer showrooms!

On balance, careers in fashion are rewarding in many ways, and your opportunities will not be limited by the lack of a college degree. The field is varied, with careers as diverse as trend-setting designer and hard-nosed buyer. In manufacturing or retailing, the possibilities are virtually limitless. As a reference point, some typical career paths are described on the following pages.

———————CAREER PATHS———————

As mentioned earlier, careers in fashion merchandising can be divided into two general categories — manufacturing and retailing. Careers in manufacturing include fashion illustrator/designer, sales representative, and product line manager. It all begins with an idea.

Fashion designers are the creative force in manufacturing. Starting with a "look," designers create all kinds of apparel to set that particular style. Some years ago, for example, the Annie Hall look was in. You could buy no pants but baggies, and tie manufacturers marketed to women for the first time. Every detail of a garment is styled to fit an image. Great attention is paid to details like pleating, cuffs, tapering of lines, etc. The best experience for this kind of work is fashion illustration, which just happens to be where most designers start out.

Fashion illustrators are a specialized type of commercial artist. Working from a designer's notes and rough sketches, the illustrator completes the look with color and detail. Lapel widths are determined, as are hem lengths and button styles. Garments are accessorized to flatter the design (belt not included). Illustrators gain valuable experience in translating concepts onto paper, learning about A-line and empire waists, sweetheart and boatneck collars and double breasted and cardigan style jackets. Good fashion illustrators command good salaries, earning $30,000 a year and more with a few years experience. Most important, they are the first considered for designer jobs, where compensation can reach six figures for top people.

The goal of fashion illustration is to make the designs most attractive, because they are used as a kind of product advertising. Illustrations appear in studio and store catalogs as well as fashion magazines, where customers (individuals and/or store buyers) see them and decide to buy or not to buy (that is the question...). Illustrators must have not only good drawing skills but also a feel for how fabrics flow, what are the most flattering model poses and how to accessorize a garment for best effect.

Not to be confused with illustrators are pattern makers. This unique group of people is responsible for drawing clothing patterns from which garments are actually cut and sewn. Pattern makers must take into consideration not only different measurements for different sizes, but also how different fabrics and materials cut, what kind of seam allowances must be made and other crucial factors in manufacturing. Pattern making is one of those jobs nobody notices when it is done well, but all hell breaks loose when it's wrong. Good pattern makers are highly sought after, and since garment making is such a closed industry, everyone knows everyone else and where they work. An experienced pattern maker in a high fashion market may make $30,000 or more. There is not much upward mobility, however, and today's pattern makers tend to be older. Those who retire are seldom replaced.

Of course, even the hottest designs do not sell themselves. Unlike the retail end, where customers come to you, manufacturers take their products to the customer (the retailer). Sometimes this is done by sales people employed by the manufacturer, but more often independent representatives are used. There are several advantages to this system, chief among which is the representatives knowledge of the marketplace. Reps, or agents, sell more than one line (so long as they do not conflict), and thus get a lot of "backdoor" business. That is, they establish a line of belts, for example, in a certain department store. Their relationship with that store buyer then allows them to introduce another product, say gloves. Also, the reps usually are paid strictly on commission, which means that a manufacturer pays only when and if the agent produces.

Careers in fashion "repping" tend toward the entrepreneurial. Most agents have small operations, employing perhaps three or four salespeople to cover certain territories. Many reps work as individuals, controlling completely their lines and accounts. Either way, there is never a dull moment. Reps are always hustling, soliciting new accounts and products. This type of work requires strong product knowledge, as well as intimate familiarity with the local market. Reps must determine the best prospects for their lines, and concentrate their efforts on those areas. The best fur coat line in the world will not sell in K-Mart. It is hard to estimate rep income, since it depends so heavily on performance, but good reps can bring home $40,000-60,000 or more a year.

Supervising the reps are product line managers, who work directly for the manufacturers. These product managers are responsible for a certain product, or group of products, and do everything possible to maximize that product(s)' success. Product managers train reps, make sales calls with them, pass on sales leads, provide product samples to interested prospects, negotiate special pricing for large deals, monitor store displays of their product(s), develop sales strategies for new styles, and generally move those shoes (or ties or whatever). Naturally, the job requires in-depth product knowledge, as well as knowledge of the marketplace and competition.

Product managers often do a lot of traveling, working long and hard to achieve the best possible market penetration. They interview and sign on new reps, train their personnel and make "buddy" sales calls. At night, they review call reports and record their expenses. It's tough work, but the effort is rewarded, with experienced product managers earning $35,000-$50,000 a year in salary alone. Usually there are commissions and/or bonuses involved too. Top product managers move up to district, regional and finally national sales or marketing directors, where incomes are well over $100,000 a year.

The retailing end of merchandising is equally lucrative and exciting. Careers in retailing range from store buyer to Inventory Manager, display designer to department head. Let's look at the process from start to finish.

A retail store must of course have products to sell, and how many of what kind is determined by the store buyer(s). The buying season begins a full year before merchandise will actually sell in the stores. It starts perhaps in January with trips to fashion shows and designer showrooms, seeing what is being offered at what price. Some purchases are made right on the showroom floor. More often, a buyer will narrow his or her choices down to a group of items and invite representatives to show them the lines in more detail. By now it is April. Some negotiating takes place, and deals are made. Selected items are shipped to a department store's warehouse sometime in August, to be delivered to retail outlets around November. The swimsuits will appear on the racks right after Christmas, at which time it is impossible to buy wool coats anymore. Like magazine publishers, clothing stores are always ahead of the season, a situation that results in retail salespeople sweating in the latest mohair sweaters in August.

In addition to buying styles of items, buyers also determine how many to bring in when, what sizes and colors, etc. Supplementing large yearly purchases are the periodic specialty items peddled by the reps. Often such items turn into the hottest sellers, perhaps because they catch trends when they're current, rather than six or eight months after the fact. Thus buying is a never-ending cycle of shows, negotiations and purchases, and it can be a grind. The money is good, though, paying $40,000 to $65,000 at the top levels. And there is the excitement and glamor of it all (not to mention the designer outfits available at cost.)

Once products are brought in the goal naturally is to sell them. Many people contribute to this effort, starting with the display designers, whose job it is to put merchandise where it will catch the customers' eye and still be in reach of their arms. A good display will also generate additional sales, suggesting outfits and combinations to coordinate with a pair of pants or a vest. What's a new suit without a tie? In addition to window and mannequin dressing, wall displays are put together, hopefully featuring the higher profit items. Display people may be employed by one store, or move around among locations in a chain. Compensation is usually in the area of $25,000-$35,000 a year, more in New York City, home of Macy's, Saks, Lord and Taylor and the $10.00 hamburger.

Experienced display people often move into store design positions. People in such positions are responsible for laying out entire stores, determining how much space to give which items. This attempts to be an exact science, with each square foot of store space expected to generate a set amount of revenue. In addition to window and wall displays, store designers select and lay out display cases, choose carpet and wall coverings, and generally set the tone of the store. Usually such people work in the larger chains, hopping from one location to another, particularly when new outlets open up. A store designer can earn $40,000 a year or more, with a lot of company-paid travel to boot.

Finally, spearheading the effort to move product are the floor salespeople. With a year or two retail sales experience, you should move into an assistant store manager position, possibly a department head in a larger store. Department managers are responsible for hiring and training salespeople, scheduling work hours, authorizing merchandise exchanges or returns, keeping the racks neat and well stocked, and most importantly, selling the goods. It normally is the manager's job to decide when items need to be marked down and by how much. This is a key decision. A great deal of money is lost when items are discounted before the largest possible number have sold at full price. On the other hand, no money at all is made if something never sells. Then, too, the manager must consider the "opportunity cost" of the item; i.e, the value of the rack space it is taking up. Would something else sell better? Should an item be put on sale sooner to make room for a new, potentially hot seller? Decisions, decisions.

Store managers also have fiscal responsibilities such as keeping sales and inventory records, working within a budget, controlling shrinkage (shoplifting) and reconciling the day's transactions. More on retail management careers is given in chapter 11, Retail and Restaurant Management Careers, but for now, I will say that an average store manager earns $20,000-$35,000 a year, depending on the store and location. Often, there are performance bonuses as well, and the chance to move up further still, where the money is very attractive indeed.

SPECIALTIES

Like many of the other careers in this book, fashion merchandising has its own specialties, and most people become adept in certain areas more than others. Usually, this takes the form of concentration in a particular product group, such as menswear, accessories, outerwear or children's clothing. Look through the classified section of any large newspaper and you will see ads not for department heads but Better Sportswear Department Managers, not store managers but Maternity Fashions Store Managers. Employers will pay for your expertise, but at the cost of limiting your marketability.

Also under the fashion umbrella are such things as cosmetics, toiletries, personal accessories like wallets and sunglasses, jewelry and home accessories like linens and china. These are all areas in which people specialize, learning the products and buzzwords, studying the competition and the marketplace. Once you have spent four or five years in one area, you are an expert, like it or not, so be sure you get into an area you like before you put down roots. If you can't stand children, for heaven's sake get out of infant sleepwear!

There are some miscellaneous fashion merchandising specialties — not defined by product group — worth mentioning briefly. One is trade show specialist, a job designed to drive you crazy in a hurry. People who organize trade shows thrive on stress, work best under pressure and always seem to have a mouthful of pins. Fashion organizers do it all, soliciting participants, scheduling display times, hiring models, renting space, arranging refreshments, zipping up jumpsuits, advertising the show, printing invitations, contracting valet parking services and dabbing out pizza stains seconds before a model is due on the runway. It's exhausting, nerve-wracking and exhilirating, all at the same time. Other possibilities include wholesaling, off-price and factory showroom merchandising.

Whatever niche you carve out for yourself, an added benefit of selecting fashion merchandising as your career is that you can begin now. Many high school students work part-time and/or summers as salespeople in department and clothing stores. Although for most it is simply a paycheck, for you it can be valuable experience for your fashion career after graduation. There are also ways you can prepare educationally, and in the following section, we will look at both courses and practical work experience you can get now.

PREPARATION

Careers in fashion are unique, and require specialized skills. While great emphasis is placed on style and flair, above all, fashion merchandising is a business, with the same systems and demands found in other industries. The best preparation, therefore, is to take as many business courses as possible while you are still in school. If you are already out, sign up with a local business school to study basic accounting, inventory methods, etc. It's not a bad idea to learn a little typing, too, if you plan to work in the front office.

In addition to business, of course, there is the design end of it. Like commercial art, fashion design careers can be accelerated by formal study of your craft. There are a great many fashion design schools from which to choose. Yours should emphasize basic drawing skills, with special attention paid to such things as proportion and movement. You should also learn about the use of color, actually working with different patterns and materials. Like other trade schools, the best ones employ instructors who work in the business. They have their fingers on the pulse of current industry trends and demands, and make great references when you get out in the real world. Be sure to get letters of recommendation before you leave.

A good two-year fashion design program program can cost $3000 or more. However, most offer flexible day and evening programs so that you can work while you attend school. It is unlikely that an entry level fashion position would offer any tuition assistance, but if you can find the money, a design school can be a good career investment. By no means is it a necessity.

Most designers start out as illustrators, and while the top fashion studios may require degrees, there are many other places to start. Department and specialty stores hire illustrators to prepare work for their catalogs as well as ads for the fashion magazines. Another often overlooked area of opportunity is the sewing and crafts market. Magazines like *Butterick* and *Vogue Sewing* (or *Knitting*) use illustrators to show what a finished pattern should look like.

It is quite possible to land one of these these entry level jobs without spending a fortune on design school. Just be sure you learn as much as you can where it's free — in high school. The same courses useful to commercial artists will serve you well, too. By all means take drafting and fine arts classes. I would also recommend sewing (good old Home Ec). Much of what makes good fashion design comes from a knowledge of fabrics and materials. Learn about silks and taffetas, linens and lambswool. Put your education to use as soon as possible in a practical work environment.

The most obvious (and common) place to gain practical fashion merchandising experience is on the floor of a department or specialty store. As mentioned earlier, the key to this type of experience is to not treat the job as only a paycheck. Indeed, you might be grateful that entry level openings are so plentiful in fashion. That is not the case with most good careers, and you would do well to make the most of each opportunity. This means doing more than the minimum. Take the time to learn about your products. Examine new arrivals. Note which items move quickly and which are repeatedly discounted to no avail. Make yourself available to customers, helping put together outfits, finding the right sizes, etc. You will learn a lot more than your colleagues who sit behing the cash register chatting or reading magazines, and you will be noticed.

Although little or no experience is required for sales clerk positions, it is still a good idea to start part-time or do summer work before you graduate. This will put you a step ahead of other applicants with no contacts who must walk in off the street and fill out applications. Also, with a little experience, you can pick and choose where you will work full-time. There may be no difference in pay, but some stores are definitely more desirable than others.

The other entry level department store position mentioned was stock clerk, and here too it is possible to work part-time and summers. Particularly during peak seasons, the stores are always looking for help in receiving, inspection, sorting, stocking and various other inventory tasks. As in entry level sales, the important thing to remember is that your job is not simply a job, but the first step on the road to your fashion career. Show an interest in the garments. Make the extra effort to match each shipment against the packing slip, and packing slips against order sheets. Inspect display racks periodically and replace items as they are sold. Keep a good mix of sizes and colors out front. Ask questions and learn. You will be recognized.

Aside from retail work, there are other ways to get practical experience in fashion merchandising, though you may not be paid for them. These include volunteering your services to charity groups in organizing fashion shows, craft exhibits, etc. Theatrical work in costume design and wardrobe selection is also good experience. All in all, any opportunity to get your hands into fashion will be useful to your career. If you do not sew, learn how. At the very least, you should be able to follow pattern directions (like baste and stitch), know right and wrong garment sides, be able to calculate yardages with and without nap and understand basic pattern proportions. These may seem like unnecessary details, but they are the stock and trade of your profession, and you will do better for knowing them, especially without a lot of formal education.

The most important way to prepare for a career in fashion merchandising, or course, is to love it. The hours can be long, the work grueling, the pressure tremendous. But the rewards are there, and to stick it out through the rough times, especially in the beginning, it helps to truly enjoy what you are doing. In truth there is a lot to love. Fashion merchandising is exciting and often glamourous. There need never be a dull moment. Above all, it is up to you to make a success of it, and when you think about it, that's a pretty nice kind of business to be in.

6

Finance

Many people are familiar with the quotation from St. Paul "Money is the root of all evil." In fact, St. Paul never said those words. What he said was "The love of money is the root of all evil." Nonetheless, the finance professions have remained somewhat tainted through the years. Today, when it is once again patriotic to make a profit, accounting people are derisively referred to as bean counters. The insinuation is that such people merely calculate profits, while others do the real work of earning them. If they only knew!

Business as we know it today would be completely impossible without the involvement of finance professionals. From general ledger and cost accounting to auditing and tax planning, it is the financial people who turn revenues into profits, making sure there is something left after Uncle Sam takes his share. Not only do finance and accounting involve a whole lot more than numbers, the actual figure work is not as cut and dried as you might think.

Today's corporations, and the laws governing them, are so prolific and complex that deciding how to work the numbers is as important, if not more, so than the calculations themselves. When is a sale a sale? When an order is booked, goods are shipped or payment received? How should the value of inventory be figured? How should the cost of capital equipment be debited? In one lump sum, or over the life of the equipment? What about depreciation? There are any number of perfectly legal ways to do these and other things, and it is the finance people who determine what is in the company's best interest.

Not all accounting is done after the fact, however. Financial people, from accountants who determine the total cost of bringing a new product to market to those who decide what can be charged for it, have tremendous influence in the business planning process. If the second figure cannot be made larger than the first, only a fool would make such a product. Certainly a company would want this information beforehand. In the merger mania that has gripped American corporations recently, financial people are more involved than ever in analyzing the balance sheets of potential targets, arranging financing, or plotting strategies to make their own figures unattractive to hungry raiders. In America, at least, money does indeed make the world go 'round, and it is the financial professionals who do the spinning.

Finance, or accounting, as it is also called, has two distinct sub groups — general ledger and tax accounting. Within general ledger in particular are many different job opportunities for non-degreed applicants. Careers in accounts payable and receivable as well as general ledger, cost accounting and auditing offer great opportunities to candidates with no more than a high school diploma, a good head for figures, a willingness to work hard and learn, and the ambition to succeed in a terrific career. The potential is unlimited and the possibilities varied. Let's look at some typical careers.

PEOPLE IN FINANCE

Though nothing may be certain in life but death and taxes, a great many people and corporations cannot resign themselves to the latter. Because the government has obligingly created ways to avoid taxes — if you are clever enough — tax accounting is a booming profession. The game is simply to keep one step ahead of the tax laws. Thus a great portion of a tax accountant's time is spent reading new tax laws as they come out. This happens literally every day, not only for federal taxes but state and local ones as well. A subtle variation of this game is trying to predict what changes will be made, so that a company (or individual) can act before a new law goes into effect. At the time of this writing, for example, the federal government is considering eliminating the mortgage deduction for second homes. Since property purchased before the law goes into effect is exempt from it, many accountants are advising their clients to buy this year if they intend to buy at all. Indeed, many people will make no financial decisions whatsoever without consulting "my accountant," and by that they mean their tax accountant.

Individual tax accounting is only one part of the business, however. Tax accountants work for corporations and CPA firms, too, advising businesses how to minimize their collective tax bills. The role of a corporate tax accountant is not merely to know the laws, but to know how to use them to his company's best advantage. This requires an in-depth knowledge of the entire operation. A tax accountant must take into account capital expenditures so that they can figure deductions for depreciation. Corporate investments must be reviewed to determine capital gains and losses. No stone is left unturned in the search for lower tax bills (and thus higher profits).

CPA firms (Certified Public Accounting firms) use tax accountants for much the same purpose. The difference is that the accountant works not for a corporation but for an independent consulting firm (the CPA firm). CPA's are contracted to clients for all kinds of financial work, including tax returns advice and preparation. Generally, careers in public accounting require not only a finance related degree but additional study and passage of a multi-part state exam not unlike bar exams in law. It is, however, possible to get started without a degree, and learn as you earn.

The other main branch of finance is general accounting. This term covers a great many areas, including accounts receivable and payable, cost accounting, payroll and internal auditing. The most "general" of the general accounting careers is general ledger.

A ledger, of course, is a book in which credits and debits are entered and tallied. Credits are positive cash transactions, like customer invoice payments. Debits are negative transactions, like the company's payment of its own bills. Today most of this is done on a computer, but general ledger accounting still is referred to as "keeping the books." GL accountants usually oversee AP and AR people as well as bookkeepers, who do the actual entering and balancing. The GL accountants themselves are more concerned with monthly and yearly budget planning, implementing new accounting systems, reviewing contracts with customers and other business related duties.

Another distinct area of general accounting is cost accounting. As the name implies, cost accountants are concerned with what things cost, primarily things which can be charged to specific products rather than general overhead. In corporate finance, every expense must be "charged" to something. This includes not only purchased goods like paper clips but also employee time, machine time, the building space any given department occupies and that department's share of lighting and heating costs. Every penny must be accounted for somewhere. The job of the cost accountant is to calculate the charges involved in producing a given product or service.

To do this, cost accountants must analyze the entire manufacturing process, from the cost of component parts to workers' time and wages. Nothing is overlooked in calculating the total cost of a product, and that is merely the first step in a longer process. Once costs have been determined, they must be reduced. Somehow, in the eyes of management, at least, costs can always be reduced, and most times they are right. Work processes are analyzed in detail. Would a new machine eliminate the need for 2 employees? At what cost? Would cheaper material suffice? If it breaks easily and increases waste, how much, if anything, is really saved? The answers to these and other cost questions are vital in determining pricing structures, profit margins and even whether to make a product at all. As you can see, cost accountants have a profound impact on the companies they work for.

Lastly, we come to auditing. By this I do not mean Internal Revenue Service auditing, a process corporate auditors work very hard to prevent. Internal auditors work for either corporations or CPA firms, and are responsible for reviewing all financial records and procedures. This is necessary not only to maintain internal control of the books, but also because most corporations are publicly held, and are ultimately responsible to their shareholders. Numerous and varied reports must be filed with the Securities and Exchange Commission, which tightly regulates member companies. The job of internal auditors is to ensure that proper procedures are consistently followed, and the necessary information available to be scrutinized.

Internal auditors usually work for large companies and travel frequently from location to location, reviewing a division's financial records for a few weeks and moving on. In addition, publicly held firms usually hire independent agencies (CPA firms) to audit their books, and certify that they have used legitimate accounting procedures in preparing their financial statements. In the past this has largely been a formality, but in recent years shareholders have been filing and winning suits against CPA firms which audited corporations found guilty of misrepresentation or malfeasance.

It should be obvious at this point that careers in finance are as varied as they are challenging. Each type of accounting has its own career path, and each begins with certain junior responsibilities. Let's look now at some typical entry level jobs in finance.

THE ENTRY LEVEL

Entry level jobs in accounting are relatively easy to come by, degree or no. It is a profession in which there seems to be constant demand for good people, and there generally is a lot of on-the-job training provided. A common way to break into accounting is as a figure clerk in an area like payroll or billing.

Billing clerks are responsible for issuing invoices on the first of the month, preparing customer statements, making credit adjustments, keeping aged trial balances and sundry other duties. In billing you will learn about things like 2% 10, net 30 terms of payment, F.O.B. points and account aging. Initially there will be a lot of clerical work, typing (or printing) statements, filing confirming purchase orders, preparing credit memos and the like. As you gain experience you will begin to handle problems with customer accounts and shipping companies, establish terms of credit for new customers, authorize credits and put accounts up for collection when necessary.

For all of this you should expect to earn between $13,000 and $15,000 a year to start. In addition, many companies offer tuition assistance. You should take advantage of this. Taking business and accounting courses, in addition to your work experience will qualify you for promotion as higher positions become available.

Another typical entry level accounting job is payroll clerk. Responsibilities in payroll vary greatly depending on how automated a company's systems are. Most larger companies have computerized their payrolls, which eliminates the manual calculation of employee hours worked, multiplied by rate of pay, minus tax percentages and other deductions, etc. Even when this is all done automatically, though, there always seem to be adjustments to make; for example, when an employee forgets to punch out one day or doesn't get overtime pay authorized.

Even when all goes smoothly there is plenty that must be done by people. In particular, monthly and quarterly tax deposits must be prepared and filed, disability and profit sharing checks figured and distributed, bonuses and commissions paid, etc. Today many companies have their payrolls prepared by outside services. There are good reasons for doing this, not the least of which is keeping salaries and other payroll information confidential. While this has eliminated some jobs with corporations, more have been created with those service companies, and you should definitely consider them as potential first job opportunities.

Entry level payroll jobs should pay between $12,000 and $15,000 a year at first. Again, make use of any tuition assistance offered to enhance your job skills and move up in the accounting department.

Perhaps the most common entry level accounting job is bookkeeping. Bookkeepers are responsible for "posting to" (making entries in) the general ledger, keeping petty cash records, doing trial balances, balancing bank account statements and issuing checks. At first your duties will be those of an assistant, maintaining customer files, reconciling the petty cash drawer at week's end and finding errors in account totals. With enough experience (usually when you can work an adding machine without looking) you will begin to make final ledger entries, close out the books at the end of the month and authorize payments.

Bookkeeping is a more complex job than many people realize. It is not simply a matter of running two columns, one for credits and one for debits, though eventually it is reduced to that. Long before that stage, debits must be charged to proper departments within the company. These decisions are not made lightly, nor are they often straightforward. For instance, data processing time is often charged to the "user" department, but who pays for the printer paper and tape? Where are charges for office cleaning and security services applied? There is no one right way, but once a system is chosen, it must be used consistently.

There must also be a distinction made between cash balances and ledger balances. For purposes of keeping the books, credits and debits can be counted when they occur. For example, a sale may be "on the books" when it is invoiced. Often that is when salesmens' commissions are paid. The bank, however, is not likely to cash checks against invoices, and running cash totals must also be kept. In bookkeeping, you will quickly learn about all different types of money, and that depending on how you figure it, your company can be swimming in either cash or red ink. If you ever discover why it takes two weeks for checks from a bank next door to yours to clear, please let me know.

Bookkeeping jobs should pay around $13,000 or $14,000 a year to start. Try to start with a company which does most of its accounting by computerized systems. Not that this will make your job any easier; in some ways, it will be more complex. But computerization is the wave of the future, and the day is not far off when the lack of computer skills will be as debilitating to your career as not speaking English. The earlier you begin working with automated systems, the better. In addition, your computer skills will increase both your marketability and your salary level.

In tax accounting, the most common entry level job is preparing tax returns. There is no law which says you need a degree to do this. In fact, most tax services like H & R Block employ housewives and students to prepare returns. They are given a few weeks' training, mostly familiarizing them with basic forms and legal deductions, and sent into the lions' den in January. By April, these people are old pros. Some can do a short form return in twenty minutes. Others twist paper clips and cry at loud noises. They are all very tired by the fifteenth of April.

Of course, at first you will be responsible for minor things like breaking out FICA, witholding, and state and local tax amounts, entering standard and fixed deductions (like personal exemptions) and actually filling out return forms. If you work for an accounting firm, you may later become involved in figuring interest deductions, business expenses, depreciation allowances, investment tax credits and income averaging. These are all things you should learn, but do not continue to believe the common myth that tax work occurs once a year.

For one thing, many small businesses as well as individuals use accounting firms to prepare their taxes, and businesses operate on varying fiscal years. For individuals, the tax year begins on January 1st and ends on December 31st. The following April 15th, you have to pay up. Businesses, on the other hand, can choose their own tax years, perhaps starting September 1st and ending August 31st. Their money must be in by the following December 15th, four months after the end of their tax year.

Furthermore, many small businesses use accountants to prepare their monthly and quarterly payroll returns, handle unemployment compensation forms and payments, file necessary insurance papers, etc. Thus, tax accounting is a year-round enterprise, with responsibilities that include not only federal and local tax return preparation but keeping financial records, learning the latest tax laws and applying them to the client's best advantage and — God forbid — handling government auditors.

Entry level jobs in tax accounting vary in rates of pay. A tax service like an H & R Block will pay little more than minimum wage, but will be good experience, and may be the only way you can break into the field. An accounting firm, on the other hand, may pay $12,000 to $14,000 a year to start. There you may have broader responsibilities than simply preparing annual tax returns, and there will be greater opportunities for career advancement.

All of this may sound pretty humdrum. If you always have thought of finance as a dull way to make a living, I have told you little so far to change your mind. Creative accounting, if there is such a thing, is usually a euphemism for something illegal, and is generally frowned upon. Attention to detail is of paramount importance; accidentally dropping that last "0" is no small matter. There is not a lot of room for experimentation, or trying things "your way."

And yet all is not grim. The finance department has tremendous impact on corporate decisions, as well as the bottom line. Accountants, for all their "button-down" mentality, are respected for their command of the numbers, and few people can argue as persuasively as a finance officer armed with graphs and charts. As advisors, accountants are revered on a level with doctors, and people consult them with the same deference. Many a deal has been soured because "the accountant does not recommend that move at this time." Finally, accountants are well paid for their services, and they have responsibility far beyond that of people in other departments at similar job levels, as we shall see in the next section.

CAREER PATHS

As mentioned earlier, careers in finance fall into two general groups: general accounting and tax accounting. Most opportunities for non-degreed candidates are in the general accounting area, so we will look at those careers first.

The most common career paths in general accounting are those that lead to full charge bookkeeper. Starting as an accounting clerk, you will progress through accounts payable and/or receivable into management in one of those areas. This will be your first opportunity to exercise supervisory responsibility. Manager of Accounts Receivable, in particular, is a highly visible position. Your activities will have direct and serious impact on the corporate bottom line.

Especially in today's economic climate, celebrating landing a big contract is premature to say the least. Making a sale is all well and good, but it now seems that collecting monies due is an equally arduous task. The longer a customer can avoid paying your invoices the longer they can live off your money. When we are talking about millions of dollars, the difference between paying in thirty days and seventy five days adds up to a lot of interest the customer does not have to pay on borrowing that money from a legitimate source. You cannot afford to play banker to your customers, and it is your job as Accounts Receivable Supervisor to manage invoicing, account aging and collection when necessary.

You should expect to spend 3-5 years in an intermediate level management position, where you should earn between $18,000 and $22,000 a year. Once you have sufficient experience, you should start to look for a full charge bookkeeper opportunity, either with your present company or elsewhere. In such a position you can expect to make $30,000 a year or more, depending on the size of the company and your particular skills; e.g., familiarity with computerized systems, etc.

An alternate career path is one leading to Credit Manager. Again starting out as an accounting clerk, potential Credit Managers work their way up through positions of increasing responsibility, usually over a period of four to six years. Like Manager of Accounts Receivable, the Credit Manager's successes (and failures) are evident to all, as they impact significantly on corporate profits.

The main responsibility of the Credit Manager is to make the job of Accounts Receivable easy. That is, by thoroughly referencing a customer's credit status, collection problems and the need to write off bad debts can be minimized. Of course, credit problems cannot be avoided altogether. Many large, reputable companies are notoriously slow in paying, or experience temporary cash flow problems which stretch their accounts out beyond sixty or even 90 days. The only sure way to avoid credit hassles is to sell on a cash only basis, and that's pretty hard to do when your business is heavy equipment or other "big ticket" items. However, good credit control definitely can prevent a lot of problems down the road. The Manager of Credit is in a position of tremendous responsibility.

Not only do Managers check out new accounts, they also control the open balances of existing customers. Just because a company was rated AA when they opened their account with you, or still are rated highly, does not mean all is well. There is a fine line between accommodating a good customer in a tight period and throwing merchandise out the window. A great many people were left holding the bag when such solid companies as Storage Technology and Financial Corporation of America went bankrupt. A good Credit Manager continually evaluates his customers' account statuses. He or she must make decisions about terms of payment, freight charge assessment, credit limits and when to take a customer off open account. This is all very delicate; no company can afford to alienate major customers by not shipping critical merchandise, and yet it does no good to make sales on which you cannot collect. It's an unpleasant job at times, but somebody's got to do it, and you'll be well paid for your efforts.

Credit Managers with a few years experience can expect to earn between $20,000 and $28,000 a year. Salaries vary greatly based on the size of the company. Larger companies have substantial credit departments, where the Manager may supervise four or five assistants, as well as clerks, secretaries, etc. Smaller operations may have just the one Manager, who has direct responsibility for controlling customer account status.

Still a third career possibility is a career in internal auditing. As mentioned earlier, internal auditors usually work for larger corporations, where they are responsible for reviewing all financial operations. Not only is this required of publicly held companies, it is a good check on a company's accounting procedures. Auditing the books has been known to turn up suspicious irregularities, but more often, internal auditing is used to evaluate the efficiency of a company's operations.

A manager of Internal Audit usually has 5-7 years auditing

experience, and is responsible for managing all auditing personnel. This includes selecting, hiring, supervising, motivating and evaluating the junior people, reviewing their reports and making recommendations to corporate officers on ways to better manage the company's finances. Unlike cost accountants who study and evaluate operations to make them more efficient, auditors are concerned with financial reporting methods and procedures. The Manager of Internal Audit is ultimately responsible for the accuracy of all financial statements, verifying not only the numbers but the methods used to produce them. It is an awesome responsibility, and auditors generally are well compensated, earning $25,000 to $33,000 a year with some experience. The Manager of Internal Audit may make up to $45,000.

Careers in tax accounting are a little more limited for non-degreed applicants, largely because most full-fledged tax accountants work for CPA firms, where they must be state certified. While it is possible to achieve this without an accounting or business degree, it is quite rare. I would not recommend pursuing that course of action. The tests are designed for accounting program graduates, and the programs are designed to prepare students for the exams. Why fight the system, especially when you can get started in tax preparation without a degree?

If you are serious about a career in tax accounting, but do not have the desire or resources to spend four years studying the tax laws full-time, your best bet is to work for an independent tax service. There you will gain experience, learn a lot about the tax system and make enough money to eat and go to school at night. The only other way to progress in tax work is to strike out on your own, and many have done this, very successfully.

As I said earlier, there is no law which requires tax preparers to have accounting degrees, and many owners of preparation services do not. While you will not be asked to file for IBM, there are plenty of small businesses as well as individuals whose tax situations are not so complex that they require Alexander Grant to figure them out. H & R Block is probably the most well-known service, but the majority of Americans who have given up filing for themselves go to small local outfits. There's a lot to be said for the entrepreneurial life. Tax preparation is particularly well suited to a home occupation, though it can become as big a business as you develop it to be.

It's hard to say what kind of income to expect. There are many variables in owning your own business, and operations vary from one person services which only work during "tax season" to large offices handling hundreds of clients year round. With some experience, contacts and a lot of effort there is no reason you cannot be successful in your own tax business. At the very least you'll know how much to deduct for your home office (den) and employee's (spouse's) salary.

SPECIALTIES

Like so many other professions, financial people usually develop specialties at some point in their careers. In finance, this generally takes the form of specialization by industry, both in tax and general accounting.

Tax accountants, degreed or no, usually specialize in handling accounts within specific industries. This is because the tax laws have become so complex that is impossible for any individual to know or even know of every existing tax, not to mention how to avoid it. In the oil industry, for example, special allowances are given for resource depletion, credits are given for investment in certain types of exploration but not others and so on and so forth. Similarly, real estate taxes are a field all their own. So is transportation. Overall, tax professionals specialize or die. A fringe benefit of this is that established tax services get a lot of additional business as a result of referrals from satisfied customers with friends "in the industry."

In general accounting, specialization occurs in the general ledger as well as cost area. Special laws govern the management and reporting of finances in such industries as insurance, health care, publishing, high-tech electronics and farming. General ledger accountants must become versed in the proper procedures for their respective industries, not only to prepare reports correctly, but to take best advantage of what the laws allow. Similarly, cost accountants can figure expenses many different ways, depending on the requirements of any given type of business. It goes without saying that auditors, too, must learn the systems and procedures peculiar to the industries in which they work.

In addition to specialization by industry, some miscellaneous financial specialties include asset management, commission accounting, research and development costing, international trade and nonprofit corporation accounting. As always, your knowledge and experience in finance will open the door to many related careers in such areas as sales and marketing. Independent payroll services as well as financial software producers are hot for accountants with communication skills to represent their products in the business marketplace. Furthermore, a background in finance is ideal preparation for a broader career in business management, where the potential for advancement is virtually unlimited.

All of these heady career possibilities begin with a down-to-earth attitude of hard work and honest preparation. There are no short cuts to success, not even college. No one in their right mind would entrust the company cash to a greenhorn, no matter how educated. Everyone has to learn the ropes, and the time to start is now.

PREPARATION

Finance is a career for which the average high school offers a lot of opportunity to develop the necessary skills, beginning in the class-room itself. Of course you should take as many math courses as possible, with special emphasis on those with practical value. Many schools offer business math and even introductory accounting classes. By all means take them. Just as important is learning the basics of computer systems.

I cannot stress enough the importance of becoming familiar with computers. Even the smallest companies are "going on the compu-ter," mainly because it is so darn easy today. There are so many excellent off-the-shelf financial software packages on the market today that almost no company writes their own financial applica-tions software anymore. For you this means that you need not become a programmer, but you certainly had better learn to use some basic systems. Computer skills are a giant plus, and the lack of them is an even bigger minus. A lot of older people in accounting would give their eye teeth for the chance to develop computer skills free of charge. Make the time to learn some basic computing tools. You will be well rewarded for it.

As far as practical experience is concerned, a lot of the same activities as those recommended in banking apply here too. Get involved in the business end of school projects. Volunteer to serve as business manager for the yearbook. Run for class treasurer. All of these things are great experience, not only for the skills you will develop but for the discipline as well. Learn early on to pay attention to detail, question things which don't seem right to you and above all, plan ahead. In accounting, there is no such thing as close enough . Figures must be worked and reworked, meticulous records kept and hard questions asked.

Outside of school, there are not too many places to exercise your skills. You might get a summer job as a figure clerk somewhere. Good experience and references, too. Mostly, though, your first full-time job will be your first paid experience, which is okay in finance. There is plenty of opportunity to learn on the job, and if you work hard, pay attention to everything going on around you, take on responsibilities and do the little jobs well, no one will care whether or not you have an expensive piece of paper claiming you can do the job. You will already be doing it.

Of course, if your company offers educational assistance, by all means take advantage of it. There's always something to learn, and I'd be the last one to say there won't come a point in your career when a degree will be an asset. Either way, your career in finance can be exciting, lucrative and rewarding. It takes work, determination and a clear focus on your goals, but the potential is real, and should you decide finance is for you, you won't be disappointed.

7

Nursing

Of all the careers discussed in this book, perhaps the one offering the most opportunity is nursing. A combination of factors has created a critical shortage of qualified nurses nationwide, especially in the larger metropolitan areas. Demand for nursing professionals has increased dramatically over the past 5-8 years, as evidenced by page after page of classified job advertisements in local papers. And good nursing opportunities will continue to exist for the foreseeable future.

Why, you may ask, if nursing is such a great career, is there such a shortage? Shouldn't people be lining up to get into a good thing? The answer is yes, and they are doing just that. Today's shortages are the result of an unprecedented number of nursing drop-outs in the recent past. Partly because nurses were not properly respected or compensated, partly because of the women's movement (which urged nurses to "raise themselves" to doctors), and I'm sure for other reasons, too, many experienced nurses simply quit to do other things. The timing was such that hospitals and other health care institutions currently are feeling the pressure of nurse shortages, and are hiring in record numbers.

At the same time, the nursing profession is coming into its own as a respected and vital field of medicine. Primary patient care, long considered "custodial," is now justly regarded as an essential element of treatment. Many hospitals have developed systems of nurse/patient interaction in which a patient is assigned the same nurse on each shift throughout his stay. For the patient this means better care in that nurses are better able to chart progress, detect minor and generally be better informed about a particular patient's condition. For nurses it means more satisfying involvement with patients and a new role as an important participant in treatment planning as well as implementation.

Perhaps for some of the reasons listed above, more and more men are considering nursing as legitimate careers. Where previously male nurses may have been ridiculed, or used nursing as a stepping stone into a "real" medical profession, today men, as well as women, recognize and exploit the tremendous opportunities nursing has to offer. And they are tremendous!

Not only is there fantastic demand for nurses, opportunities in the profession today are almost limitless. Of course, the major career areas are in patient care and will rightly remain so. But experienced nurses also work in research, education, occupational health and publishing. Even within patient care (or clinical nursing), there is more to consider than the standard hospital shift work. Medical services today include preventive medicine, rehabilitation, mental health care and many other non-traditional types of treatment in which nurses are needed. Each of the many areas of opportunity offer its own challenges and rewards.

PEOPLE IN NURSING

The vast majority of nurses work in what is called clinical nursing, or primary patient care. This is what most of us think of when we picture a traditional hospital nurse in white hat and shoes. Responsibilities are varied, and can be awesome. Hospital nurses are the first level of contact between treatment and patient. If you have ever been hospitalized, you know that visits from the doctor are few and far between. Even when they do visit, they tend to spend most of the time consulting with your nurse(s) about your condition (Has his fever come down yet? Does he still have stomach pains?) This can be annoying, especially when they talk about you as though you were not there, but there is very good reason for your doctor to talk to your nurse as well as to you. Nurses do not simply administer treatment, they supervise it. That is critical, because each case of pneumonia is as unique as each person is.

Of course, doctors take into consideration a patient's age and medical history when prescribing treatment. But "medical condition" is a dynamic thing, and it is the nurses who monitor reactions to drugs, recommend dosage changes, and measure the effectiveness of prescribed treatments. Just as important is the nurse's role in explaining treatment procedures and goals, possible side effects, etc. It's a lot less frightening to have the room spin around you when you have been told the drugs may make you feel that way. Conversely, if you know that a certain pill is supposed to alleviate the pain in your side — and it doesn't — you know to speak up.

Another large part of clinical nursing is the dreaded paperwork. Nurses at times seem to swimming in a sea of charts and folders, surfacing now and then to make notations. Some of it is excessive, especially the flood of forms that must be filled out for insurance purposes. However, most of it is truly necessary to properly monitor, record and later review degrees of treatment success or failure. Such records also become a vital part of a patient's medical history. And so you most definitely will need to pay meticulous attention to detail, keep records current and organized, and know how to correlate data from different charts, graphs, X-rays, etc.

Not very much of this sounds like Florence Nightingale comforting the sick and tending to their needs. It's hard to know how much of the traditional nurse image ever was true, but I can say that today there simply isn't time for much "tending" (which is mostly done by nurse's aides now). Even in fully staffed institutions, a nursing shift is crammed full of "rounds" (dispensing medication and administering other treatment on set schedules), tests, record-keeping, consultations and emergencies. It's a constant struggle to get it all done, let alone with a smile and a song. And yet all is not sterile.

It has long been recognized by parents (and nurses) that tender loving care is often the best treatment for coughs and colds. Even with more serious illnesses, attitude is an important factor in recovery, and it cannot be denied that a happy patient heals more quickly (and often more completely). Recently, "the medical profession" has come around to this same conclusion, heralded with all sorts of scientific study and test results Thus a good "bedside manner" is once again considered a vital part of nursing, and can be the most personally satisfying as well.

For those who find institutional nursing too impersonal, despite the advent of primary (one-to-one) nursing, there is plenty of "private duty" work available. Private duty nurses are licensed or registered nurses who provide care in a patient's home. This is also considered clinical nursing in that it involves direct patient care, but in private duty work there is the opportunity to develop relationships with patients and provide more good old-fashioned TLC. Of course, you also supervise and administer treatment, and the responsibility is even greater than in a clinical setting. Not only are in-home doctor visits less frequent, emergency equipment is not available, and the importance of watching a patient's condition very closely is greatly magnified.

While most nurses work in one or another clinical area, there are also many other support and educational opportunities in the nursing field. Most related to "core" nursing are such fields as occupational health and school nursing.

Occupational health refers to nursing in the workplace. Most large companies have some type of health center for employees, where basic medical care is given in case of accident or sudden illness. In this type of work, there is the additional responsibility of diagnosis, something done by doctors in clinical settings. You will also administer required treatment, though naturally anything serious (or possibly serious) will be referred to a local hospital.

Some companies offer more extensive health services, including things like diet and exercise programs, and psychological services such as family and stress counseling. Here your role would be more that of a consultant, reviewing an individual's medical history, recommending a fitness program best suited to their needs and monitoring progress. Employees benefit from improved health and well-being; employers benefit from better work attendance and higher productivity. This type of nursing falls under the umbrella of preventive medicine, a field which is growing by leaps and bounds today.

School nursing is similar to occupational health in that a lot of the job is diagnosis and referral. However, like any medical field devoted to the care of children, special pediatric training is required, as is a placid temperment. There are also unique pressures involved, namely from parents, ranging from over-protective mothers who want to take Billy home every time he sneezes to the sad fact of abusive parents. There is, though, special satisfaction of working with youngsters. School nursing is a popular field.

Finally, a large and important field in nursing support is education. Nursing schools are staffed by experienced and specially trained who devote themselves to educating future generations of nursing professionals. Nursing education is more than work in the classroom, though coursework is vital. Instructors also supervise laboratory training and first experiences with actual patients. Since medicine is such a dynamic field, nursing educators must keep abreast of new procedures, techniques, drugs, etc. They are able to do this with the help of those toiling on the other side of the medical education field; i.e., textbook publishing.

Like any academic discipline, nursing requires its own course material. Who is better qualified to prepare it than nurses? Publishers must agree because experienced nurses are being hired in record numbers to write, illustrate and edit nursing textbooks, workbooks, tests and other classroom material. Medical journals and trade magazines also employ nursing writers and editors. The medical publishing field in general is exploding with opportunity, and nursing in particular has taken off. There are unique demands and rewards in any type of education, and if you are attracted to them, be aware that there are lots of ways to use your nursing background to get into that field.

As always, no one starts at the top. Nursing in particular has a rigid advancement structure, based partly on education and certification, partly on experience. Once you are licensed or registered, though, there are very definitely some universal entry level responsibilities. Let's look at entry level nursing in some detail.

THE ENTRY LEVEL

Nursing is the only career in this book which requires more than a high school diploma to get started. You cannot work at any level in nursing without certification, and you cannot become certified without going to nursing school. Nor can you work in the field, say as a nurse's aide, and go to school part-time. Nursing school is a full-time affair. Between classes, lectures, laboratory and hospital work, there simply is not time to do much else. In any case, nurse's aide jobs are really not good preparation for a nursing career, and they pay so little that the income would be little help anyway.

Entry level nursing jobs, then, are filled by full-fledged nurses, be they licensed or registered (there is a difference which we will discuss later on). Depending on what area of medicine you are in, responsibilities vary, but all entry level nurses are greenhorns. Though your license may say you are qualified to work as a nurse, most institutions want you to prove it, and beginning "staff" nurse jobs can be grueling.

Almost all entry level jobs are in clinical settings; i.e. institutions like hospitals, nursing homes, rehabilitation centers, etc. For one thing, this means shift work. Due to the nursing shortage, it is no longer true that junior nurses automatically start on night shift, though you may want to for the substantial bonuses many hospitals offer. You will, however, work weekends for sure. It is a fact of life that patients require care 24 hours a day, 365 days a year, and nurses must be there to provide it. Even experienced nurses work weekends, though not as many holidays; it comes with the territory.

Beginning staff nurse responsibilities usually consist of doing rounds, doing rounds and doing rounds. Other times you will do rounds. As discussed earlier, "rounds" refers to giving patients treatment at set intervals. Treatment may be a pill, a shot, a sitz bath or a massage. When you are not making rounds, you will be doing a variety of odd jobs, things like transporting patients from surgery to recovery, taking patients for special tests or "logging" (making entries on patient charts). You should expect to spend a good two years as a staff nurse, learning different procedures as well as hospital routine.

What do entry level nurses earn? The picture today is much brighter than it was just a few years ago, when nursing was considered another "women's" job, with commensurately low pay. Today, your first nursing job should pay between $15,000 and $18,000 a year in a nursing home or other residential care facility, more in a hospital. These figures are for registered nurses (RN's). Licensed practical nurses (LPN's) should expect to make around $14,000 to start. LPN jobs are fewer in number as well.

However, nursing is not a career one chooses for the money. The other careers discussed in this book certainly offer other rewards in addition to financial ones. Nursing, though, is unique. For one thing, it is the only non-business related career included. Hospitals and nursing schools are non-profit institutions, and as such, there reason for being is completely different than say, an advertising agency. The medical "business" is not without ambition and greed, but nursing at least is a purely service profession. The demands and satisfactions are unique, and so is the environment.

It goes without saying that to be a nurse you must truly love helping people. Many of your "professional" responsibilities, especially in the beginning, will involve some pretty unpleasant tasks such as cleaning patients who have soiled themselves, bathing invalids, etc. I wish I could say that patients are universally grateful for your services, but alas, they are not, or at least they don't show it. Most of the time, you must be able to gain satisfaction from knowing that you have made someone a little more comfortable.

And then there is the pressure. Most of the other careers in this book involve pressures of one kind or another, be they meeting deadlines, making budgets or what have you. Believe me when I say these pale in comparison with the pressures involved in the medical field, where mistakes or "missing deadlines" can cost lives. Today more than ever, nurses are feeling the pressures of their very weighty responsibilities. Not only must you live with the consequences of your errors, you will more than likely be destroyed by a malpractice suit if you do not have insurance (which threatens to increase beyond the means of most medical professionals). It is a sad fact that a growing number of nurses are leaving the field because of these pressures, directly or indirectly.

Finally, no discussion of what it's like to work as a nurse would be complete without examining the emotional pressures of the job. Patients die. Despite your best efforts, and those of the entire medical team, people still die. Contrary to popular opinion, nurses and doctors do not "learn to live with it." Every lost patient hurts. The key to staying sane in such an environment is how you deal with it. I honestly don't know how most nurses manage, especially those who work with terminally ill people. It just is not the sort of job you can leave at the office. I'm pretty sure that a lot of it is balanced by one's "successes."

I have, so far, intentionally painted a rather bleak picture of the nursing life. Considering that most people get their images of nursing from soap operas, where the nurses spend most of their time fighting off doctors in the supply room, I thought I should let you know what you're getting into. If you're still interested in the job, you deserve also to know that it can be tremendously rewarding, too.

Just as the pressures are greater and the lows are lower, the highs are much higher than any you experience in other careers. What can compare with helping another human being return from serious illness or injury to a healthy, productive life? Even with "hopeless cases," you have the satisfaction of knowing that you have made their last days or weeks as comfortable as possible. On a personal level, nurses and other health professionals belong to that lucky group of people who have a reason to get up in the morning. Even the most exciting and rewarding job in business is just that — a job. As a nurse, it really does matter whether or not you go to work tomorrow. And that can make it all worthwhile.

The icing on the cake is that nursing can be pretty rewarding on a career level as well. From Nursing Director to Instructor and Laboratory Supervisor to Textbook Editor, nurses enjoy exciting (and lucrative) career opportunities. Let's look at some typical career paths.

CAREER PATHS

Careers in nursing can fall into one of two general groups — direct patient care and support services. Almost all nurses start out in patient care, and a great many remain there for their entire careers. Beginning as "staff nurses," new entrants spend 2-4 years performing the general responsibilties discussed in the "entry level" section. With four years' hospital experience, you should be earning around $23,000 a year, and should be looking for opportunities to move up to an assistant supervisor position.

As an assistant supervisor, you will begin to have some managerial responsibilities like scheduling personnel hours, reviewing patient records and consulting with your department head on serious or ambiguous cases. At this point, you may want to take advantage of your hospital's tuition assistance program (almost all of them have one) to go back to school part-time for your Bachelor of Nursing degree. This is by no means required; many successful high-level nurses have no more than their registration. It can definitely be helpful, though, and it is free (or very inexpensive), so think about it.

After 3-5 years as an assistant supervisor, where you should earn approximately $28,000 a year, you are qualified to be a Department Head.

The Nursing Head of a hospital department, say Pediatrics, has tremendous responsibility, beginning with personnel. The Department Head recruits, evaluates, hires, trains and supervises all junior personnel in the department. At larger hospitals this can be twenty-five nurses or more. In addition, the Department Head has many administrative responsibilities, including setting and meeting budgets and representing Nursing at hospital planning sessions. For all of this, a Department Head can expect to make $30,000 to $35,000 a year, more in larger metropolitan areas.

The pinnacle of institutional nursing careers is Director of Nursing. At large hospitals, reaching this position can require 12-15 years nursing experience, as well as advanced education. Salaries are impressive, reaching $45,000 a year and more. Smaller institutions, like nursing homes and residential centers for the handicapped, may have only twenty nurses on the entire staff. There the functions of Department Head, Supervisor and Director are combined, and it is possible to become Director of Nursing at such a facility in about eight years. You should expect to make $28,000 to $35,000 a year as Director of a smaller institution.

A somewhat different direct care career path is that of nurse practitioner. This is a relatively recent job title which has developed into a very popular career option over the past 10 years or so. It is especially appealing to those nurses who want to advance in their profession, but at the same time don't want to give up direct involvement with their patients. Previously such people had little choice, unless perhaps they had the means and ambition to attend medical school. Today they can become nurse practitioners.

Basically, a nurse practitioner is a nurse who has undergone additional training, primarily in the area of diagnostic skills. A Bachelor of Nursing degree is required, as well as certification to work as a nurse practitioner. Usually practitioners work in public clinics or treatment centers rather than hospitals. The most common areas of opportunity are in pediatrics and obstetrics/gynecology, where nurse practitioners perform physical examinations, make diagnoses and recommend treatment for minor problems. They also do a lot of counseling in areas such as nutrition, hygiene and family planning. Technically they cannot prescribe medication, and any serious or potentially serious problems are referred to a medical doctor. However, in most other respects, nurse practitioners enjoy the advantages of private doctors in that they can develop relationships with their patients over the years, and advance their careers without losing touch with the reason they became nurses in the first place.

Experienced nurse practitioners are in great demand, and can command salaries of $30,000 a year or more. There is also the advantage of more regular hours, though supervisory nurses in institutions are usually exempt from shift work, too. Most of all, as a nurse practitioner, you are better able to serve patients, many of whom may never see a doctor except in a hospital emergency room. You are their lifeline.

Careers in support services are equally diverse and rewarding. Probably the most common nursing career outside of clinical work is that of office nurse. Private physicians employ nurses to do a variety of functions, including interviewing new patients, taking medical histories, doing laboratory work (such as blood and urinalysis) and checking vital signs (blood pressure, temperature, etc.). In addition, there are a lot of administrative duties not found in hospital nursing. As an office nurse, you will become intimately familiar with things like third party providers, covered services, allowable charges, and other insurance mumbo-jumbo. You will also have such clerical responsibilities as answering phones, scheduling appointments, typing prescriptions, mailing bills, etc.

There are a lot of advantages to working in a private office, not the least of which is sane working hours. Then, too, office work is neater, more organized and less demanding emotionally. Certainly there is a lot less pressure. However, demand in this area is not as great, and salaries do not often exceed the $20,000 to $22,000 range.

Another area of opportunity is nursing education. Obviously, someone has to teach nursing. This can be a very rewarding profession. The qualifications for instructors are usually a Bachelor of Nursing Degree (BSN) and several years nursing experience, preferably in a supervisory capacity. Unlike many academic disciplines, work experience in the field is considered essential background for instructors. This is because not only do they teach in the classroom, but they supervise "lab work" (work with patients) as well.

Nursing Instructors, happily, do not suffer from the same low pay scales as teachers in other disciplines. This is probably because anyone qualified to teach nursing is already earning more than many college professors, and would hardly be attracted to teaching if it required a cut in pay. Experienced full time nursing instructors can expect to make $26,000 to $30,000 a year, more with tenure and/or department supervisory responsibility. Many nurses continue to work in the clinical field and teach part-time, enjoying the best of both worlds, as well as handsome incomes.

On the other side of education is textbook publishing. There has recently been an explosion in demand for qualified nursing textbook writers, editors and illustrators. Perhaps because of renewed interest in the profession, which has swelled the ranks of nursing students, opportunities have never been better for nurses with writing or drawing skills. Usually a nurse entering publishing will begin as an editor, reviewing articles or chapters for technical accuracy or updating new editions of old textbooks. With some experience, you may move into actually writing a textbook chapter or journal piece on an area of your expertise. Above all, you will be expected to keep current on new developments in the nursing field, scanning periodicals for news of new techniques or procedures, discoveries of new treatment side effects, etc. The plan is that your technical expertise will insure that accurate and current information is presented. How it is presented, that is, literary style, usually is left to lay editors.

Nonetheless, publishing can be exciting and rewarding. It is certainly the most business-oriented area of nursing. You are working with a product which has deadlines and sales figures to meet. You'll work closely with illustrators and authors. In magazine publishing, you will have a great deal of influence over which articles are published and who writes them. For all of this, you can expect to earn $22,000-28,000 a year or more. Many nursing editors work on a free-lance basis. There is more than enough work available, and rates go as high as $20 an hour.

Some opportunities in support services include laboratory research, personnel recruiting, hospital equipment and pharmaceutical sales, temporary nursing agency management, and state licensing. The market couldn't be better for qualified nurses. Whether you choose clinical nursing or an area of support service, opportunities are everywhere, particularly in certain specialties, discussed below.

SPECIALTIES

Like doctors, most nurses specialize in one or another branch of medicine. Almost any field requires nursing assistance, including internal medicine, obstetrics, surgery, cardiology, neurology and geriatrics. Some areas in particular offer great career opportunities for today's nurses.

One such growing field is pediatrics, the branch of medicine devoted to the care of children. Pediatric nurses work in hospital neonatal units, doctor's offices, clinics and schools. There is a unique talent in diagnosing illness in patients who cannot communicate where it hurts. Another unique talent is handling frantic mothers, determining which phone calls require the doctor's assistance and which require calm words. In hospitals, some of which are entirely for children, nursing can be heartbreaking. There is nothing sadder than losing a child, which makes the ones you save all the sweeter.

Another large area of specialization is surgical nursing. These are the ones glorified on "Ben Casey," and rightly so. Surgery is one of the most grueling and pressured fields of medicine, in part because it can be so unpredictable. Emergency operations can be required at all hours of the day and night, and it is not only the doctors who must respond. Nurses are a vital part of the surgical team, and complex operations can require the services of 5 or 6 nurses, even more. Responsibilities vary from keeping a watch on vital signs to providing the required instruments. For most surgical procedures, which are non-emergency, the nurses' job begins long before the actual operation.

First the required instruments must be selected and sterilized, then arranged properly. Also the patient's condition must be constantly monitored to determine reaction to anesthesia. Even after the surgical procedure has been performed, many times the doctor will leave an experienced nurse to "close," i.e., stitch up the incision, bandage, etc. Then a nurse must accompany the patient to recovery, watching their condition closely for signs of difficulty. All in all, surgical nursing involves a lot more than wiping Dr. Welby's fevered brow.

A third area of clinical nursing which presents a lot of opportunity is emergency room work. Here you will find a little of everything. On any given afternoon, an emergency room nurse may handle a heart attack case, an automobile accident victim, a child with food poisoning, an unexpectedly sudden infant delivery, a burn victim and a construction worker with a severed hand. All of these are clearly emergencies and must be handled immediately, but some order must be established, and it most definitely is not first come, first served. A large part of an emergency room nurse's job is what is called triage. Triage means determining what action needs to be taken immediately in any given case, and which cases need the doctor's attention first. If a pint of blood will hold a patient over until the doctor is through with another one who has stopped breathing, that is what you do. It's an extremely high pressure area of medicine. Few nurses stay in the emergency room very long, but it is excellent experience. If you can do that, you can handle anything.

Finally, a growing branch of medicine with a lot of opportunity for nursing professionals is psychiatry. Recently it has been discovered that many "mental illnesses" have physiological causes, and can be effectively treated with drugs. Psychiatric hospitals employ nurses to administer and monitor treatment, take patients for tests, etc. In addition, many psychiatric patients tend to be disoriented and frightened, and it is the nurse's job to explain treatments and side effects to those who can understand them, disturb a patient's routine as little as possible, and generally make their therapy as comfortable as possible. This type of nursing can be uniquely satisfying, as few diseases are as disabling or affect the patient's family as greatly as psychiatric disorders. Returning a mentally ill patient to health is a thrilling experience.

Any of these challenging and rewarding fields can be open to you with the proper education and skills. Unlike the other careers presented, nursing alone does require additional education after high school. However, you do not need a four year, or even a two year degree to get started, and you can begin to prepare in high school. Let's look now at how best to prepare yourself for a career in nursing.

——————————— PREPARATION ———————————

As a field of medicine, nursing is a science. As such, you would be well served by taking as many science courses as possible in high school, especially biology and chemistry. Physics is not as important, and I would recommend another chemistry course instead, particularly organic chemistry. Math courses are also essential, with special emphasis on algebra. All of these will put you in good stead when you get to nursing school, where you will study more of the same, as well as sociology, psychology and other humanities.

The next decision is where to attend nursing school. There are a lot of choices. Many hospitals have two or three year nursing programs, as do community colleges and universities. If you go to a regular college, the clinical part of the program will be given in affiliation with a local hospital. There are a number of things to consider when making this decision, not the least of which is cost.

If you are really strapped financially, and cannot manage a full-time two year program, many hospitals offer a one year course leading to certification as a Licensed Practical Nurse (LPN). Unless it is the only way you can swing it financially, I don't recommend this. LPN's are not state registered, and legally cannot do many of the things RN's can. As such, they are not as much in demand, and do not earn nearly as much. If you want to become registered later on, you will still have to do another year full-time, so you might as well get it over with in the beginning.

Among programs leading to registration, there are two, three and even four year degree courses available. As a general rule, college programs run two years and hospitals three. It used to be that many students preferred hospital programs because as graduates, they were favored for entry level jobs with the hospitals they attended. Today there are more than enough jobs for beginning nurses, and you might as well look for the most for your dollar, which will probably be the local community college.

Two year community college nursing programs generally cost about $3000, including lab fees, materials, uniforms, etc. Financial assistance is available from a variety of sources, and student loans for something as practical as nursing should not be too hard to obtain. With your salary you should have no trouble paying off the loan in short order. Private college nursing programs can run $3000 a year or more, and hospital courses are even higher. It makes sense to do the first two years as inexpensively as possible, and go the private college route for your BSN later — at your employer's expense.

Graduation from an accredited two or three year nursing program does not automatically qualify you to practice nursing. The programs are designed to prepare you for state certification, which involves a series of tests given by your state's licensing board. While most people pass, the tests are not a formality, and should be taken seriously. Once you are registered, you are eligible to work as a nurse anywhere in the state, be it a hospital, doctor's office or clinic. The doors of opportunity to a fabulous career are open!

Nursing today is more challenging and rewarding than ever. No longer considered doctor's handmaidens, nurses enjoy the respect of the medical profession as well as personally satisfying careers. What's more, you will be well paid for doing something you love, and you will know for certain that one person *can* make a difference.

8

Publishing

People have been predicting the extinction of publishing since the advent of silent movies. Radio and television spelled certain death for literature, the same pundits intoned. Well, here we are, well into the video age, and reading is still the great American pastine. In 1984 alone, more than 50,000,000 books were sold. Countless others were borrowed from libraries and friends. (Some were even returned!) The point is that reading, and therefore publishing, is back in vogue, if indeed it was ever "out."

I'm not just talking about the great American novel, though fiction is deservedly popular. Tremendous markets exist for non-fiction and trade books, reference works, anthologies, children's literature, how-to books, cookbooks, biographies and hundreds of other publishing categories. Big publishing houses are prospering and small and specialty presses are sprouting up all over the place. And when they are not reading books, Americans are likely to be leafing through one of the latest magazines.

Even more so than book publishing, the magazine industry has embraced the specialty markets, with fantastic success. A new magazine competing with *TIME* and *Newsweek* has little chance, but by addressing special interest audiences, issues like *Micro Age, Country Living, Science Digest, Barron's* and *Boating Magazine* have carved out nice little niches for themselves. In the same way, scholarly journals like *The Harvard Business Review* and the *Journal of American Pediatrics* are flourishing.

All of this means that publishing today offers many challenging and interesting career opportunities. Indeed, the most wonderful thing of all about the resurgence of publishing may be that you can not only benefit from it, you can participate in it. Exciting and rewarding careers in publishing are open to non-degreed candidates with ambition, talent and the right preparation. Like so many of the "creative" professions, what matters is your ability and determination, not the letters after your name. Not that you can breeze right into the top levels of publishing — you can't. Even landing an "Administrative Assistant" job with a good publisher can be tough. However, plenty of non-degreed people have successful careers in a variety of publishing areas. Let's look at some typical ones.

PEOPLE IN PUBLISHING

There are really two distinct types of publishing — magazines and books. Of the two, magazine publishing probably represents the better opportunity, especially for beginners, if only because there are more magazine publishers. Furthermore, unless you live in the New York City area, there are not very many book publishing houses large enough to consider.

How, then, are magazines produced? As you might expect, it all starts with the money, which magazines bring in from subscribers, newstand sales and advertisers — mostly from advertisers. Even Literature with a big "L" is big business these days, and magazine publishing is even more closely tied to revenues. Thus, people in magazine publishing work in circulation, advertising sales and other business areas.

The Circulation Department is responsible for soliciting new subscribers and making sure that old ones renew regularly. Strong subscription numbers are vital to a magazine's success; indeed, many special interest publications are sold only through the mail. Subscribers are the financial base of a publication. Management knows that they can count on selling "X" number of copies to subscribers every month, which helps set accurate production figures. Furthermore, subscribers pay for their years' worth of *Scientific American all at once in advance*, which improves a publisher's cash flow situation tremendously, and allows him to offer typical subscription "savings of 47% over the cover price."

Perhaps even more important than actual subscription revenues are the rates healthy circulation figures allow a magazine to charge its advertisers. Rates are determined by readership; obviously an ad which is guaranteed to reach 500,000 consumers is worth more than one read by only 200,000. These numbers are all the more critical when you consider that the great majority of any magazine's income comes from advertising, and that fees based on points and market shares — like those in T.V. advertising — are often used to set prices.

Once there is enough money for an issue, you need material to fill it. Enter the editors and artists. I often think there are as many kinds of editors as there are months of the year. Editors can be Contributing editors, Assistant Editors, Managing Editors, Department Editors and even editorial editors. In other words, they can be Writers, "Gofers," Supervisors, Real Editors, etc.

Contributing Editors are queer ducks. What they really are are writers who have had their work published in a particular magazine over a period of time. They cost the publisher too much money as free-lancers, so they are made part of the salaried staff. In return for a weekly check, they write a certain number of pieces for the magazine as they were doing before, with the main difference being that topics for articles are suggested by the publisher as well as by the writer. Very rarely do they get involved in what we would consider editing anything other than their own work. If what is on the newsstands is any indication, many do not even own dictionaries.

Department (or Articles) Editors and their Assistants do the things we think of when we think of editing. That is, they wring their hands in anticipation of receiving articles from sensitive young writers, which they will savagely denigrate, gleefully hack and slash and ultimately reject. Worse yet, they may accept a piece, tormenting the author through months of harsh criticism, ridicule and rewrites. All for eight cents a word. Only a Hemingway could make a living.

Actually, Editors and assistants are the writer's best friends, helping him to tailor his piece to the magazine's needs, offering suggestions to improve both content and style, proofreading the final draft and going to bat for the writer when there are differences of opinion with upper management. Believe me when I say that magazine editors genuinely want to publish promising articles. Though their offices are literally flooded with submissions, only a tiny fraction are well-written, in the proper format, at the right length, at the right time and suitable for the magazine. Anything with any sparkle and/or relevance at all will be given more than a fair chance.

So . . . . now we have money to put out a first class magazine and enough material to make it dynamite. This is not the end, nor even the beginning of the end, but the end of the beginning. If Winston Churchill had submitted those words to *Life* magazine they would have come out "This is the end," thanks to those wonderful people in Production.

In production, space is truly the final frontier. All those terrific articles and pictures have to fit into this month's allotted 120 pages somewhere, hopefully without too many "cont. on p. 92, col. 3"'s. Production is responsible for the layout and arrangement of each issue, and must consider both aesthetics and costs. Advertising and copy must be balanced, artwork produced and set, galleys printed and the pages run.

Of course, as a business like any other, magazine publishing also employs people in finance, advertising, personnel, data processing and office services. Even in these ancillary departments, I'll bet it's fun working for *People Magazine*. That would be the choice of many. For me, it would be even more of a kick to work for a big publishing house like Harper and Row or Doubleday.

Book publishing is another animal entirely, mainly because the major source of a book house's revenue is product sales rather than advertising. It really matters to the bottom line how many copies a book sells. What's worse, selling books is harder because there are no residual sales. Where the same guy who bought January's issue of *Sports Illustrated* likely may buy February's, book buyers are not loyal to any particular house. Imagine an ad for a new novel touting it as "from the publisher who gave you that bestselling thriller *Claws*." Who cares? A following for an author, maybe, but a publisher? Perhaps it happens in some specialized non-fiction categories, but for most new books it's back to square one so far as marketing is concerned.

With so much riding on every new release, the book editor's responsibilities are great, beginning with manuscript selection. Submissions must be considered not only in terms of merit but marketability as well. Publishing houses usually specialize in producing certain types of books, and it is not financially rewarding for them to bring out totally unrelated books, not even those destined to become classics in our own time. Even promising manuscripts are often rejected if an editor feels that too much time and effort would need to be invested to bring the material up to an acceptable standard. Unlike magazine publishing, it is often thought better to publish nothing at all than something "risky."

The risks can be great indeed. It is not simply that a publisher does not make as much money on a book that sells only 15,000 copies as he would on one that sold 50,000. If they had planned for that book to sell 15,000, *and priced it accordingly*, it might even be a success. However, a planned 50,000 seller with sales of 15,000 actually loses money. This is because of set-up costs.

The single most costly factor in publishing any book is making the plates from which it will be printed. Therefore, a book must sell a minimum number of copies, depending on the selling price (wholesale), to pay off the plates. Only then is any profit made. On the other hand, money spent on plates for slow movers might as well be thrown out the window, as it can never be recovered.

The flip side of this, of course, is than once plate costs are recovered, it's all gravy. Paperback reprints and new editions of existing works are especially profitable, which is part of the reason it is so hard for new and unknown writers to get published today. Why take a chance when easy money is available? It is ultimately book editors who determine what chances are taken, and once they decide to take a chance on some poor writer, heaven help him!

As much as any writer wants his work to be a success, so too do editors spend sleepless nights working and worrying over a manuscript. It becomes their baby, too. Book editors work closely with chosen authors, critiquing format and style, slaving over preliminary, intermediate, next to last and almost final drafts. A good editor's input can be invaluable, not only in terms of their writing skills, but also his or her knowledge of the marketplace. Editors are apt to know what sells, and taking a different approach or focusing on a more specific audience may make the difference between a so-so book and a blockbuster.

This kind of expertise doesn't develop overnight, nor is it possible to walk right into an editorial position. The world is full of people who want to work in publishing, and a whole lot of them could do very well at it. Not everyone will be given the chance, though, and if you want to break into the field, you will probably have to accept a starting job less lofty than Writing or Editing. Like typing.

THE ENTRY LEVEL

A large percentage of Managing Editors and Editors in Chief began their careers as editorial assistants, a title similar in nature to that of sanitation engineer. What assistants are are gofers. Usually this type of entry level job is supposed to introduce you to the greater responsibilities which await you down the career path. For the life of me I can't figure out what you are supposed to learn as an editorial assistant, certainly nothing worth the three or four or more years many talented young people spend at it. It's simply a situation where there are a lot of hopefuls and few jobs, so entry level people tend to stay entry level longer than necessary.

As an editorial assistant, you will be responsible for a myriad of little details so vital to making things run smoothly. There is a lot of typing, of course, though most of that is done on word processors these days. As a general rule, if it's handwritten, type it. If it's typed, copy it. If it's a copy, file it. And if it's Friday afternoon, forget it. In addition to typing, you will schedule appointments, prepare and mail author contracts, answer phones, verify information to be printed and send rejection notices. Occasionally, you will do some proofreading.

Proofreading is more than checking spelling and punctuation, though that is important. Assistant editors also read for continuity of style and clarity of presentation. Sentences like "We all went skiing in Al's car" should never make it past the editor's desk, not should errors in verb tense or case, poor paragraph construction or the proverbial dangling participle. Repetitive sections should be eliminated, awkward adjectives substituted and run-on sentences reconstructed. Diligent proofreading really can make the difference between a sloppy, disjointed book and a tight, coherent story.

Once a book is typeset it becomes very costly to correct errors or make other changes, so proofreaders must do a thorough job the first time around. As an editorial assistant, you will have plenty of opportunity to practice. You will learn to use and read proofreaders' marks, watch for "key areas" (errors in obvious places like section headings are most often missed) and develop some speed in your work. With time you will be able to run through a manuscript very quickly and make all necessary corrections first time around.

As dull as all of this sounds, I'm afraid there is no external compensation like a fat paycheck to console you. Entry level editorial job salaries are the pits, but what can you do? The current imbalance of supply and demand results in beginning salaries between $10,000 and $13,000 a year, maybe more in New York City. This figure is pretty constant for both magazine and book publishing. With a few years experience, you might go as high as $17,000.

Another way to break into publishing is on the business side, usually in advertising sales or circulation. Entry level jobs here are a bit easier to come by, though obviously limited to magazine publishing. In advertising sales, you will be responsible for quoting rates to customers, taking orders, processing them, meeting with production to arrange artwork, and anything else to sell space. Just as an army travels on it's stomach, so do magazines thrive or wither on the strength of their ad revenues. A publication cannot afford dollars lost in space.

Your experience in ad sales will familiarize you with things like contract time, quarter, half and full page ads, ten point type, bullets, caps, two and four color prints, camera ready artwork and in-column v. display ads. Most important, it will give you an appreciation for the importance of sound business management, something too often disregarded by the artistes in editing.

For your efforts you can expect to earn between $12,000 and $15,000 a year to start. You may also be paid commissions or bonuses based on how much space you sell. With a few years experience, salaries may reach $20,000 or more for business or other high cover price publications.

In circulation, you initially will be responsible for things like direct mail advertising (sending subscription notices), customer relations (finding out why Mrs. Delvecchio's *Soap Opera* Digest continually arrives late) and special promotions (call now and receive this desk clock as our gift). Basically, you will see to all the little details of getting new subscribers and keeping the old ones. As mentioned earlier, this is vital not only from a revenue standpoint but as a basis for setting advertising rates as well. Entry level circulation positions pay about as poorly as editorial assistantships, so if you really want to edit, start out in that department to begin with. The money is no better in circulation.

Why, you may well ask, would anyone in their right mind want such a low-paying, miserable career? Well, money isn't everything, though it gets better as you move up, and there are people who enjoy proofreading. But the real reason is because it's fun. Who never has dreamed of writing the Great American Novel, or at least a who-dunit? Who doesn't read bestsellers and think how easily they could do as well or better? Who doesn't envy Norman Mailer his fame and fortune? When you consider that the closest you may get to literary greatness is editing a famous author's new manuscript, publishing is an awfully exciting place to be.

It helps to have an appreciation for the writing itself. If you are the sort of person who gets great satisfaction from a well-turned phrase or perfect metaphor, I don't have to explain the joys of editing. The work environment is fast-paced, creative and high pressure. Where else could you spend two hours debating the merits of all fifteen John Kennedy biographies on the market, and get paid for it? Really, where else can you get paid to read a book? Most people are lucky to find enough time to read the morning headlines before dashing off to "work." Your work *is* reading.

One other thing to note about the book publishing work environment is that much of it takes place in New York City. This is a hard reality that's not likely to change in the near future. If you are serious about a career in book publishing, be aware that you eventually will have to make the big move to the Big Apple, especially if you want the big bucks. Though most nationally syndicated magazines also are based in New York, a lot of other large metropolitan areas also publish a fair number of good magazines. You should be able to develop a rewarding career locally.

Whatever you do and wherever you do it, your slugging it out in the trenches will eventually be rewarded. Then you must decide which of several career paths you wish to pursue. Some typical careers, as well as specialties, are discussed below.

─────────────── CAREER PATHS ───────────────

I can't deny that the beautiful people of publishing are the editors. Once they have put in their time at the entry level, editors begin to have some pretty exciting responsibilities. The first rung up from editorial assistant is plain old editor, or perhaps staff editor on a magazine. This is the first opportunity you will have to exercise some of that creative talent you have been saving for your magnum opus. It can also be a thankless job, where you will deal with defensive writers, surly Managing Editors and intractable production people. At night, you get to sort through stacks of "unsolicited manuscripts" ("John looked out at the green fields of his homeland for the last time . . ."). But every now and then . . .

There is that silver lining, of course; the thrill of discovering a new talent, the satisfaction of polishing a diamond in the rough and virtuously refraining from telling your boss "I told you so" when your "hare-brained idea for a science fiction mystery novel" tops the best-seller list.

An editor's workday is a long one, filled with a variety of tasks —small and large. Chief among these is working with contracted authors, defining a book or article's audience, sharpening its focus, tightening its structure, suggesting alternative approaches and generally guiding it into the final draft. At this stage there is more involved than just proofreading or criticism of style. A fiction editor must be concerned with things like plot, pace, character development and natural dialogue. Non-fiction editors critique format as well as style, check accuracy of information and organize the material appropriately. All editors look at manuscript length, clarity of presentation and suitability of material.

Many book publishers and magazines employ editors on a free-lance basis; that is, they contract with an independent editor for a particular assignment, paying either by the hour or the job. Usually free-lancers are specialists in a particular field, say medical books. They make the rounds of the medical publishers when new books come out or old ones are revised. Experienced free-lance editors can make $20 an hour or more, and have the fringe benefits of working when and where they choose, enjoying time off between assignments and being their own boss. Full-time staff editors can expect to earn anywhere from $18,000 to $25,000 a year. As always, the salary may be higher in NYC. With four or five years editing experience, you should begin to look for opportunities to move up to a Department Editor position.

In a large book publishing house, a Department Editor is

responsible for a certain category of material; for example, health and science. When manuscripts on those subjects come in, they are first reviewed by an editor in that department. If something passes the first reading, it is sent to the Department Editor for further review. They then select a chosen few for serious consideration, at which point the editor re-enters the picture, requesting additional sample chapters, sending contracts, etc. The Department Editor's decisions are based not only on the work's merit, which the editors should be able to evaluate, but on other important factors as well.

For example, your suggested biography of John Kennedy, the sixteenth to be published since his death, may well be the potentially seminal work in the field. It may also wind up in the circular file, simply because interest in the late president is only so great, and there may be little market for another bio. Timing also is important. A few years ago anything about fitness was an instant best-seller. Today interest in aerobics is well beyond the peak. Now, for some reason, cat books are big. While publishing is not an intrinsically trendy business, book Department Editors are constantly trying to anticipate the next hot topic or genre.

Magazine publishing is even more concerned with being current. Because the interval from conception to publication is shorter, magazines can be more up-to-the-minute than can book houses. Here Department Editors have publishing agendas set months in advance, but they are routinely rearranged when Princess Di grants an interview or the Mets make an unexpected run for the pennant. More so than in book publishing, magazine Department Editors often assign articles to be written, rather than wait for the right piece to be submitted. Also more so than with books, there is the constant pressure of deadlines, deadlines, deadlines. Projects which cannot be completed on time are scrapped, touching off a frantic search for replacement material But when at long last January's issue has been "put to bed," the Department Editor can sit back and reflect on a job well done, sometimes for as long as ten minutes before he is reminded that February's deadline is only twenty-nine days away.

At the Department level, editors in either books or magazines can earn $30,000 or more. The top Department heads are considered for the pinnacle of any editing career, the job of Editor-in-Chief.

In magazine publishing, there may be an intermediate position of Managing Editor, but many good Department Editors, after four to seven years management experience, move up to Chief. The Editor-in-Chief is responsible for the whole creative ball of wax, from setting the tone for the year's publishing agenda to hiring, supervising and evaluating the junior editors. They are also involved in the business end of things, consulting with production and finance to determine the number and mix of books to be published in a fiscal year, deciding how many book or magazine copies are to be run, at what prices books should sell and what advances and contract terms to offer authors It's a lot of responsibility, and top Editors-in-Chief can command salaries of $45,000 or more.

But the best efforts of the entire editing crew are for nought without the support of a first-rate publishing group. On the business side are people like the Advertising Director, Circulation Manager and the exalted Publisher. A career in magazine advertising likely will begin in sales, where you might spend 2-3 years learning the ropes, developing a client base, etc. After that, you may want to move into market research. Magazine market researchers are responsible for defining the publication's audience, discovering their interests and ability to pursue them (income), and targeting advertisers who sell to those people. There are many steps in the process, and large publications may have several people with responsibility for one or another part of the job. For example, you might design a survey questionnaire, select a group for test mailing, tabulate and correlate results and/or suggest the most likely industries and companies to target for advertising sales. Experienced market researchers can expect to earn between $25,000 and $33,000 a year.

Whether you stay in sales or cross into market research, the top of the ladder in magazine advertising is the Advertising Director. Ad Directors are not only responsible for the junior personnel in their department, they also plan and implement budgets, design ad campaigns for the magazine itself, set rates and determine the appropriateness of ad material to be printed. The buck most definitely stops at the Ad Director's desk, and a whole lot of them better show up to pay the bills. It's a tremendous responsibility, and Directors are well compensated, earning $45,000-$60,000 a year or more.

Another type of advertising is handled by the Circulation Manager. Where the ad department is concerned with attracting advertiser's dollars, the circulation people work to bring in subscriber dollars. To this end, the Circulation Manager designs direct-mail campaigns (6 months of *Barrons* for half the cover price), buys mailing lists from other magazines and product manufacturers, solicits vendors to carry his magazine and supervises customer service operations. In short, his job is to keep those subscription and renewal checks coming in. In return, the Circulation Manager's checks are very nice, with experienced Managers making $35,000 a year or more.

The pinnacle of any publishing career is, of course, the job of Publisher. In magazines, publishers usually come up through the business ranks, though in books it is often a senior editor who takes the helm. Other than an occassional "View from the Top" editorial, publishers do very little writing or even editing. Like the CEO of a company in any industry, they are concerned with long-term financial planning, operational decisions regarding magazine format (or number and type of books to bring out this year), and changes to increase circulation and/or ad revenues. Many publishers own a share of the magazine or book publishing company, but even those who do not make out well financially. It's hard to quote a range, since so many variables affect salaries, but it is not uncommon for a magazine publisher to earn six figures. Book publishers manage with about half to three-quarters of that.

SPECIALTIES

Depending on whether you work in book or magazine publishing, there are a variety of specialties you may develop. As mentioned earlier, many book publishers, especially smaller presses, tend to specialize in printing a specific kind of book, such as textbooks, non-fiction, young adult or books of regional interest. Even with a large house, you probably will become more expert in some areas than others, and will be titled according to your category (my favorite is Juvenile Editor).

Some fields are growing more than others, and you might want to consider specializing in one of them. While there's no accounting for, or predicting, popular taste, some definite trends are developing and will continue into the near future. I'm afraid that the novel is not a hot commodity, though if this is really your heart's desire, who am I to discourage you? More promising fields include children's books, popular romance, books on technical topics (e.g., computers or popular science), any type of how-to book, travel books and cookbooks. By specializing in one or a group of book types, you will develop expertise in that area, which not only makes you a better editor, it exposes you to that marketplace. You will know at a glance whether a topic has been "worked to death," and what the competition will be for books you do release. This kind of information is very important to the success of a book department, maybe as much as the quality of the books you bring out.

In magazine publishing, editors also specialize in particular areas, though their departments have somewhat different responsibilties. The head of a magazine department — for example the football editor for *Sports Illustrated* — is responsible not only for reviewing articles submitted, but more often than not assigns a staff writer or free-lancer to cover a particular story for the magazine. In this sense, magazine publishing is closer to journalism than great literature. Usually more emphasis is placed on content than style.

A large part of the magazine department editor's job, then, is to decide what is worth printing. To do that, he or she must keep current on what is happening in their field. Competing publications are reviewed regularly and closely, as are news developments. Newsmakers are pestered for exclusive interviews. In magazine publishing, there is a lot of direct competition among similar types. It is uncanny how often you will read essentially the same article in three or four related magazines the same month.

Wherever you want to end up in publishing, take heart in the knowledge that you can get there from here. The right courses and experience will go a long way toward preparing you not only for your publishing destiny, but that first break as well.

PREPARATION

The time has come for me to reveal the secret to breaking into publishing. There is in fact a magic spell which, when cast over potential employers, produces job offers. Close your eyes, click your heels three times and repeat slowly "I can type 50 words a minute, I can type 50 words a minute . . ." In all seriousness, your first job almost certainly is going to require secretarial skills. Typing is such a useful skill to have anyway, I strongly recommend you learn to do it reasonably well. If your school doesn't offer typing classes, enroll in a local business school at night. In a few months, for a few bucks, you will have a skill which will serve you well for the rest of your life.

Other ways to start educating yourself for your career in publishing are available right in your high school. The skills necessary for tasks like proofreading and editing can be developed through almost all English courses, emphasizing those which teach basic English (grammar, syntax and usage). In addition, a strong vocabulary is a definite asset. Sure, you can look it up in the dictionary, but a limited vocabulary limits the application of your creative skills.

Writing courses also are a good idea. Don't worry too much about content. Concentrate on style and clarity of expression. Rewrite a piece as many times as necessary to make it say exactly what you want it to say. Then rewrite it again to say it better. In fact, a good exercise is to edit someone else's writing, looking for ways to improve the style. I don't recommend tackling Faulkner, but a popular novel might be good. Better yet, use a non-fiction piece.

Even classes in literature appreciation have something to offer. Understanding why an author chose to express a thought a particular way will help you to evaluate how successful she was in getting the desired message across. Who did she think her readers were? How might you have said it differently? If you plan to edit fiction, learning about plot, story, pace and character development will also help a great deal in your later career.

Finally, if your school offers classes in journalism, by all means sign up. This may be the best education of all for hopeful editors. Journalism and other types of non-fiction writing are excellent vehicles through which to develop editing skills, because you won't be distracted by content and can concentrate wholly on *how* the piece is written, not what is being said. Journalism also should teach you to be a disciplined writer and editor, as great value is placed on clarity, economy of words, and good organization.

There also are many ways to get practical experience in the publishing field, even while you are still in school. Naturally you should work for your school newspaper, or at least submit articles regularly. The best option is to edit for the paper, and get some experience in evaluating which articles to print and which to pass up. What made one so much better than another? Could the rejected article be improved? How? Some schools also put out literary magazines which you should contribute to and/or edit.

Outside of school, there are all kinds of opportunities to get experience, the most obvious being to write and submit your work to some publishers. The odds of actually having something published are awfully slim, but some editors may take the time to critique your work before rejecting it. You may have a better chance with specialty or young adult publications like *Girl Scouting* or *Teen Magazine*. Make sure you do the whole job, beginning with researching which markets publish what type of material, how pieces should be submitted, to whose attention, etc. If you are fortunate enough to get published, your editor will be an excellent contact and resource person for you when you are ready to start looking for that first job.

Preparing for a publishing career is hard work, and it doesn't get any easier once you're in the race. It sometimes seems that you are competing with every English major who ever graduated from an accredited American university, as well as free-lancers looking for steady work. Just remember that in publishing, your credentials are not degrees or what you've done but what you can do. If you are willing to take whatever is available to get in the door, you've got a much better chance of being able to show your stuff when "real" jobs open up. In the meantime, work above and beyond the call, keep polishing your writing skills and stay alert for opportunities to display your talents.

It will also help to keep clearly in mind what you are going through all this for. To stick it out long enough to rise above the crowd you have to really love the work. For such a person, it isn't hard to think of a million reasons why it's all worthwhile. Discovering a fresh new talent, turning a disorganized manuscript into a masterpiece and watching that masterpiece take off are uniquely rewarding experiences in the lives of publishing people. Compared to some of the other careers presented, the income potential is not great, but it's not bad either. And think how popular you will be at dinner parties once people find out you're "in writing."

9

Retail/Restaurant Management

Retail and restaurant management offer perhaps the best career opportunities today for non-degreed candidates. A quick look through the help wanted section of any good-sized newspaper will include dozens of openings for management trainees, no degree necessary. There is such a serious shortage of qualified management personnel in these industries, that employers are making opportunities in the field very attractive. It also is very interesting work. If you just can't picture yourself sitting behind a desk for the next forty years, this may the alternative to consider.

Furthermore, if you are interested in a business career, the training programs offered by most retail and restaurant chains are among the best available. No ivory tower stuff about economic theory and the like, but practical work experience in all areas of operations and administration are provided. Believe me, you will earn that trainee paycheck. There are not many industries in which you can go as far in a business career as you can in the retail and restaurant fields, largely because the training programs are as good as they are.

For one thing, nothing could be more irrelevant to a career in restaurant or retail management than a college degree. Degreed applicants are just as entry level as non-degreed ones, with one difference — they want more money to start. Both must go through the training program; both will be just as green until they have actual "floor" experience. Employers may prefer a degreed candidate for their maturity, but then, you can be just as mature.

If you work for a chain, there probably will be opportunities for travel, and perhaps relocation to another area. Also with a chain, your career will have more room to develop. If even Chairman of the Board of Burger King isn't enough for you, there is always the option to strike out on your own by becoming a licensed franchisee. The work is demanding but never dull. Also, careers like restaurant and retail management offer the opportunity to "work with people," the stated career objective of at least two-thirds of every high school graduating class since the Johnson administration. While this often can be frustrating, and you will learn to appreciate the wisdom of whomever said "It takes all kinds to make a world," interacting with the public is also interesting, challenging and fun. If you are the type who gets a charge out of people, here's your career!

PEOPLE IN RETAIL/ RESTAURANT MANAGEMENT

Careers in store and restaurant management are grouped into two categories — operations and administration. In restaurant lingo, this is known as "back" and "front" of the house work. In retail management, it is known as operations and administration.

Operations is just that — the people and systems that operate, or run, the place. First and foremost are the personnel. In areas of service to the public, there is no such thing as a non-visible position. Indeed, the "lowest" levels of employees are the customers' first encounter with Rite-Aid. All the fancy equipment and first-class executives in the world will not bring a customer back if the cashier is rude or the store is dirty. Similarly, the restaurant with the best chef is not always the busiest. Inept waiters, dirty knives, poor parking facilities and/or over-priced menus will drive them away as surely as rotten food. Thus it is a major concern (or should be) of store and restaurant managers to attract, train and keep good employees.

You may have heard the old maxim "The customer is always right." Of course, they're not, but in service industries, this is the golden rule. As competitive as today's marketplace is, most restaurant and store personnel will jump through hoops to satisfy a paying customer. After all, if they don't the guy next door will. I have to say that this takes a certain sort of personality. Not that you have to debase yourself, but there wil be many times you will have to bite your tongue and smilingly accept a merchandise return from six months ago, or replace a perfectly good dinner platter. However, you are not paid to accept abuse, and when someone is completely unreasonable and offensive, you have every right to walk away. The goal is to take care of problems before they reach that stage.

The other thing to remember about personnel in stores and restaurants is that too often they are treated like a commodity. Rates of

turnover which would be considered disastrous and totally unacceptable in any other industry are the norm. Imagine a data processing
department where programming personnel turned over *completely*
every six months. It would be chaotic, and yet that is what goes on in
most restaurants and retail stores. This happens principally for one
reason. Management doesn't care. One teenager at minimum wage
is as good as another so far as they are concerned. There is little
incentive for a motivated employee to do beyond the barest minimum, and few are motivated to begin with. With the possible
exception of fine restaurants, personnel are like napkins, and business suffers because of this attitude. A major part of first level store
and restaurant management responsibility is personnel. Since rapid
personnel turnover and absenteeism often go hand in hand, you will
need a winning personality, a lot of patience and ten hands to get
through nights when both cooks and two waitresses call in sick.

In addition to personnel, store and restaurant managers are
responsible for inventory and cost control. "Shrinkage," a polite
term for theft and waste, is a major source of revenue loss in most
retail and restaurant operations. Shoplifting is always a problem,
but even more insidious is employee theft, a problem which is
rampant today. Then, too, a lot of product is lost through sheer
waste. When it's not your food or merchandise, it's easy to be careless,
and employees do a lot of damage to the bottom line (that's profits)
this way.

Managers try all kinds of things to control these problems. Some
are effective. In restaurant chains, strict portion control is enforced,
or better yet, set before the food gets to preparation. It is impossible to
make financial projections twice removed from point of sale when a
"large of order fries" (.99) weighs nine ounces in one location and
thirteen in another. Thus the advent of pre-measured portions in
plastic bags, which adds to costs, but is a definite improvement over
uncontrolled shrinkage.

There's not a whole lot that can be done about employee theft,
except to fire those who get caught. Most don't, though, and the cost
of those losses invariably is passed on to the customer. One interesting approach is the employee discount. Some are very generous, say
two-thirds off normal price. The philosophy seems to be that if it's
enough of a "steal," they'll buy it. It's too early to tell if these policies
are having any effect, but it sounds promising.

Shrinkage is only one part of inventory control. It cannot be stolen
or wasted until it gets there, and when and how much merchandise
to bring in is an important responsibility of first level managers. In
most chains, you can use baselines from other locations to establish
initial inventory, but every outlet is different. You may well run out

of Friendly Burgers much more quickly than the guy in Minneapolis. Worse yet, if you overbuy for Thanksgiving, you could sit on hundreds of frozen turkeys for months, taking up a lot of warehouse space and tying up a lot of cash. Usage levels are meticulously recorded, closely monitored and regularly adjusted.

The people in administration have different responsibilities and different headaches. One large area of administration is finance, and finance people in retail stores and restaurants have unique roles.

The actual cash accounting is usually done by the managers, who reconcile cashiers' drawers after each shift and match receipts against revenues (most of this is computerized now). The financial department is responsible for things like valuing inventories and other assets, balancing liquid and fixed assets and collating reports from various locations within different regions. The problem is, what is a turkey worth? Is a November turkey the same as a February turkey? How about Easter candy? Valentines' Day cards? What about inventory held by franchisees? Then there is the shrinkage issue. How much must be allowed for waste, theft and other loss? Does that leave any profit? As I say, the finance group is faced with it's own challenges, and contributes greatly to the bottom line.

Advertising is another important area of store and restaurant administration. Anywhere but America people would feel a bit silly ordering a Whopper (it takes two hands...), but thanks to those wonderful folks on Madison Avenue, we are constantly informed of what's "on sale" where and when. If it's not the TV or radio, you find flyers under your wiper blades (BIG MARTY'S FINAL CLEARANCE!!). Chains and franchisees in particular rely heavily on advertising to establish their names. Once upon a time people patronized stores where they knew the people in charge; because they were valued customers, they could count on good, consistent service and products. Today, large chains try to create this same feeling of familiarity through advertising. I don't know that anyone has ever proved the consistent effectiveness of this kind of advertising, but stores and restaurants must be big believers because they spend billions of dollars a year promoting their names.

Finally, stores and restaurants, if not their help, are very concerned with customer satisfaction. Stores especially have separate customer service departments to take complaints, resolve problems, etc. Here is where many customers find out that while Wanamakers' may think that they (the customer) are always right, the computer does not. Customer service people handle billing problems, merchandise credits, opening of charge accounts and so on. This is a very important department in any store, where customers are either satisfied or lost.

Unlike some of the other careers presented, retail and restaurant management are highly structured, and almost always begin with a management training program. Therefore, the next section will discuss not different types of entry level jobs (there's only one), but what types of training programs are available, and what to look for when you sign up.

THE ENTRY LEVEL

Basic retail store and restaurant management training programs are designed to expose new employees to all phases of the operation. You probably will spend time actually doing most jobs in the place, including cooking, waitressing, "bussing" (clearing, cleaning and re-setting) tables, selecting and receiving produce, "prep" cooking and cashiering. In a retail store, you will work the register, unload merchandise, stock shelves, take inventory, mark merchandise with price labels and close out the cash drawers at night. There are a lot of very good reasons why this type of internship is done. Indeed, from a career perspective, good management training programs can be a better investment than an MBA. Cheaper, too.

To begin with, stores and restaurants realize that new managers, whatever other experience or education they may have, are still fish out of water in their new jobs. No one can be expected to manage people doing jobs the he or she has never performed. By actually spending time cooking, cashiering or whatever, you not only will know what you're talking about when you guide an employee doing that work, you also can pitch in and help when the place is especially busy or short-handed (usually these situations occur simultaneously).

A somewhat more subtle but important benefit of doing the rounds of jobs in a store or restaurant is the appreciation you will develop for people who do those jobs day in and day out. A good manager can use this understanding not only to evaluate performance, but to develop realistic expectations of what is possible and what's not. Theoretically, two people might be able to bus every table in the place, but on a Saturday night with three parties of ten leaving together, some extra help would be appreciated.

In addition to learning the different jobs, a training program should expose you to other aspects of operation such as inventory control, customer relations and store/restaurant finances. You should observe and then assist with things like taking physical inventories, reordering merchandise, receiving, filling out income and expense reports, and handling customer complaints. Some things you will have to learn as time goes by. For example, knowing your inventory situation is useless without knowing how much breading is used to make the Colonel's chicken, and how much chicken you are likely to sell in a given period. However, you should be given the opportunity to assist the manager of a going operation, benefiting from his experience with usage and necessary stock levels.

A good training program covering the basics of the business should run at least 3 months, after which you might become an assistant manager. Entry level trainee positions pay between $12,000 and $15,000 a year to start. As an assistant manager, you might go as high as $17,000. Expect to spend 6-18 months in this position, at which time you should be qualified for your own store or restaurant.

What should you look for in a management training program? Most importantly, look for a good company you can feel good about working for. That sounds trite, but if you detest yogurt, how do you think you'll hold up working with it ten hours a day, five days a week at Yogurt Emporium? Also, I would recommend starting out with one of the larger drug, food or retail chains. Once you're through the program and ready to move into your own location, a smaller outfit might have only one opening, in Topeka. That's great if you live nearby, but if you want to avoid forced relocation, stick with a bigger operation, where there are more openings at any one time.

Another thing to consider is the level of the store or restaurant's operation within the industry. As a general rule, you're better off with an upper or mid-level chain than the cheapest of the cheap. For example, I would consider joining an operation like Marriott's IHOP (pancake house) before a fast-food chain, simply because the lowest levels of any industry are extremely competitive and there is more than usual emphasis on cost control. For example, McDonald's expects a good percentage of their trainees to wash out of the program. You will not find the same level of support from your superiors in such an environment. Then, too, your career with a very large fast-food type operation may well stagnate at the first or second management level, simply because there are so many qualified managers ahead of you waiting to move up.

Finally, a good management training program not only should prepare you for your responsibilities, but should also make clear the company's policies and positions on situations you are likely to encounter. What does the company want you to look for in a new employee? What is just cause for dismissal (not yours, one of your employees)? What is the company policy on handling complaints? How far are you permitted to go to satisfy a disgruntled customer? A free meal, or can you merely replace their dinner? At what point should you ask a disruptive patron to leave? What are you to do if you see someone shoplifting? At least one such event is sure to occur soon after you're on your own, and it's unfair as well as irresponsible to expect you to ad lib a response.

What about the environment in retail and restaurant management? Like any service business, it is one in which the best laid plans are thrown out the window when emergencies crop up — and that happens daily. Great value is placed on being able to think on your feet. Things cannot always be done by the book, and if you're short a cook, you may have to give out a few bottles of wine on the house to keep the diners from noticing that their salads have yet to arrive. Expect the unexpected and you'll always be prepared.

As "seat of the pants" as things can seem, a strong current of professionalism must underlie your actions. It's one thing to make decisions on the spur of the moment when you know the costs and consequences. It's quite another altogether to live for the moment without a thought for tomorrow. An attitude of "never mind the cost, only the best for my customers" may be fine for a Joe Namath, but too many managers like that would put a Hardee's right out of business.

At the day-to-day level, retail and restaurant trainee and management work can be grueling. Many companies work on fifty-hour weeks, either in five ten-hour days or spread out over six. You absolutely will work nights and weekends, and a lot of holidays, too. Kitchens are hot and messy, and dining rooms and restrooms get dirty (customers do not always respect public facilities). At least once a night someone will drop a bottle of shampoo in aisle seven (always the glass ones). And there will be times when you are sure the sight of one more "Chicken Delite" will make you seriously ill.

But store and restaurant management can also be good fun. There is a lot of comraderie among fellow employees, and people take a genuine interest in how you are doing. Managers who don't hesitate to pitch in and "get their hands dirty" when things get hectic are quickly accepted. Consider also — when you are up to your elbows in mayonnaise — that a whole lot of other people earn a living behind a desk, never seeing a soul all day.

Most of all, the environment in retail and restaurant management is one where hard work and responsibility are rewarded, regardless of one's educational background. Most chains have tuition assistance programs, if you become interested in further education, but you will never be turned down for a promotion because you don't have a degree. Managing a retail operation or restaurant is itself an education in life, as well as the beginning of an exciting and lucrative career.

———————————— CAREER PATHS ————————————

Once you have completed the training program and an internship as an assistant manager, you will be put in charge of your own store or restaurant. This is unquestionably the toughest step up the career ladder, and a fair number of people can't hack it. On the other hand, you can do so good a job that management will want to keep you where you are indefinitely. Both extremes can be avoided with a little perseverence and common sense.

First level managers have a tremendous amount of responsibility. The most difficult part of the job for many people is managing the personnel under them. Particularly if you are a young person yourself, you may be afraid of making suggestions to or reprimanding a long-standing or older employee. These things must be done. There is also the temptation to become "one of the guys," which undermines your authority and causes your employees to lose respect for your position. It's a fine line between a relaxed and friendly management style and being pals with the hourly help, but you must strike a balance to be effective.

Management personnel responsibilities include interviewing, hiring, training, supervising, evaluating, promoting and firing. Your company will have its policies for these things, but often you will have to rely on your own judgment. As mentioned earlier, attracting and keeping good people in retail and restaurant work is a major difficulty. You could always do worse than the personnel you have. Try everything possible to work things out with a trained, experienced person before letting him or her go.

A big part of managing the employees is scheduling their work hours. This is no simple task, not only because no one wants to work on Saturday night, but because you have to know how many people are necessary to cover any given shift. If things are slow, you can't just send a waitress home when she has planned to work that night, nor can you expect someone to rush in and work on a moment's notice if business is better than you anticipated. And you have to plan for a certain amount of absenteeism, especially during Senior week or Christmas vacation.

You should not consider yourself a seasoned manager until you have spent a good three to four years managing your own operation. By that time, you have seen it all, and should be making between $22,000 and $28,000 a year. With a large chain, your next step should be Unit Manager, where you will be responsible for overseeing the operation of several locations.

Unit (or District) managers are once removed from the day-to-day problems of getting product to the customer, and can afford to be more long-range in their thinking and planning. Usually they will travel regularly to the outlets in their area, evaluating the local managers (with a sympathetic eye, reflecting on their own experiences). In addition, they have a lot more administrative responsibilities, and must collect financial and other information from their outlets, prepare reports, attend regional meetings, meet budgets and quotas and otherwise make sure that their district contributes as expected to the bottom line. They also recruit management personnel, assign their locations and offer a shoulder to cry on when a manager's power goes out the night the Food and Drug Administration pops in for an inspection.

District Managers usually report to Regional Managers, who in turn report to Eastern or Western National Managers. As you move up in the organization, so does your income. Regional Managers earn anywhere from $40,000 to $55,000 a year, and typically are responsible for fifteen or more stores or restaurants. At the very high levels, incomes can go into six figures, with compensation including stock options, company cars, etc.

Like any industry, retail and restaurant chains employ thousands of administrative personnel as well as direct managers. These include people in purchasing, personnel supervisors, product managers, advertising and sales and marketing. Such support personnel are vital to the success of any operation, and these are good career opportunities for non-degreed candidates, too.

Restaurant chains, for example, buy tremendous quantities of food and other supplies, and their purchasing agents become involved in negotiating major contracts with many different vendors. MacDonald's alone buys 1% of all the ground beef purchased in the United States, and that's a lot of Big Macs. Buyers must take into account the requirements of all the locations in their area, and see that deliveries are made to the correct locations at the right time. Running out of clams can be disastrous for a Seafood Shanty. Where could you buy 200 lbs. of clams at 9:00 on a Friday night?

Corporate personnel managers are another important part of the support team. While individual store or district managers do the actual hiring, it is personnel's responsibility to recruit candidates, perform initial interviews, explain terms and conditions of employment, administer wage and salary programs, determine starting salaries and induce applicants to accept them. They also implement Affirmative Action programs and insure that hiring practices conform to the government's Equal Employment Opportunity laws. Personnel keeps employee records, approves and processes raises and promotions and handles employee grievances. In organized companies, they also negotiate with labor unions.

Advertising departments in store and restaurant chains are responsible for promoting the company name, and they are always developing new and different ways to do this. Not content with making impressions on the public via television and radio, restaurant and store chains have begun sponsoring celebrity golf tournaments, charity telethons and race cars. They are also the ones who dream up those special promotions like chicken sunglasses and beach towel night at Wrigley Field.

Product Management can be equally fun and tasteless. If you have watched, as I have, the development of the Egg McMuffin®, the Croissan'wich® and Breakfast on a Bun®, you know that the more things change, the more they stay the same. That truism notwithstanding, retail and restaurant product managers work feverishly to create the wonder product of the decade, or at least the week. Everyone strives to get a leg up on the competition, which is hard when you're running full steam to catch up. In all fairness, some things really do take off, and who knows, your brainchild may turn out to be the next Slurpee® or something equally attractive sounding.

If none of these careers appeal to you, how about becoming your own boss? Retail and restaurant management is ideal preparation for becoming a franchisee of some large chain, thus having your own business while enjoying the support of an established organization. Franchises are independently owned and operated outlets which are licensed to carry the Domino Pizza name, or whatever. They can be great set-ups for a family business, and your experience in retail or restaurant management will make you a very attractive applicant for a franchise.

The usual arrangement is that you pay a fee up-front for the license. This can range from $5000 to $50,000, depending on the organization. Obviously, you will want to minimize your investment, but it's important too to buy into an established and well known chain. Also you will have to buy your initial inventory and have enough cash to cover your payroll and other expenses for three months. Some chains also require you to pay a continuing share of your gross profit annually, to buy from certain sources, maintain a certain quantity and/or mix of inventory, etc. Franchise agreements vary greatly, but most offer some financial assistance, provide you and your employees with training, prepare your payroll for you, assist with site selection, and even buy or build your facility for you (you pay rent, of course). For many people, this is the only way to achieve self-employment, and it can be the best way, too. You have the backing of a solid organization and reap the benefits of their advertising promotions and business experience, as well as their good name. Of course some franchises fail, but a background in retail or restaurant management gives you a definite advantage. If you always have wanted your own business and can make the investment, by all means give it a shot.

All of the many exciting and lucrative careers in retail and restaurant management are open to you with no more than your high school diploma. You will, however, be competing with a lot of college graduates as well as other qualified candidates, and you would be well advised to start preparing for your management career now. There are several ways to do just that.

PREPARATION

From an educational perspective, there aren't a whole lot of courses designed to prepare you for the business world, but I would recommend business math, and economics if it is offered. The best thing you can do in school, however, is participate in a lot of extra-curricular activities which will show a prospective employer how well-rounded you are (business managers seem to be a lot like college admissions counselors that way). It is a good idea to get involved in student government or athletics . . . do something. Nobody wants to hire a nerd, especially for a position in which he or she will have to deal with the public. Activities not only look good on your résumé, they may really open your eyes to the big wide world out there.

Outside of school, I would suggest joining your local Jaycee chapter. The Jaycees are an organization of young business people who become involved in community projects like running carnivals for the volunteer firemen or organizing paper recycling drives. They take complete responsibility for their businesses, learning a lot in the process. The chapters usually are sponsored and run by local business leaders who volunteer their time and expertise, and who can be excellent contacts and resource people to use in your job search.

There are also a number of part-time and summer jobs to pursue which can provide you with good experience in the industry. Obviously you can flip burgers in a fast-food joint, but try to look for something where you can get experience dealing with the public. Cashiering and waiting tables are good; besides, the tips aren't too shabby. Be sure to get written references from your supervisors, and ask about what management training programs the company offers. Then look up your old boss when you graduate.

In the retail field, working as a sales clerk, cashier or stock person are all possible ways to get some experience and earn a little extra cash in the bargain. Again, get references, being sure to perform above and beyond expectations so that you deserve a good recommendation. Definitely put in an application with the personnel office, and check in periodically for news of any trainee openings.

All in all, retail and restaurant management offer tremendous career opportunities for ambitious, business-minded young people willing to put in the effort. Entry level jobs are plentiful enough, and the work environment is one in which you can determine how far you go in the organization. The money is more than good, and the work is never dull. And if you're not a "company man," there's always the franchise option. Any way you look at it, retail/restaurant management is a good place to be.

10

Travel

Where I live, a local car dealership runs a series of radio ads in which a couple consults a travel agent about possible destinations for a "relaxing vacation." Brazil, they suggest? "Oh, Brazil," the travel agent replies, "home of man-eating plants and mosquitos the size of tanks who pick you up, suck you dry and drop you into the nearest active volcano." Hawaii, then? Hawaii is similarly disparaged. It ends up with the travel agent recommending they relax at the local car dealership where the people are friendly and helpful, because "God knows, you look terrible. You could use the rest."

This, in so many words, is what travel agents do — in a more positive way, of course. Based on their experience with destinations around the globe, they help arrange appropriate trips for clients seeking relaxation, ancient ruins, championship golf courses, skiing, great restaurants, local color or an uncrowded beach somewhere (good luck). Getting that expertise is the fun part, and though the days of free world travel and stays at luxury resorts may be fading fast, travel people still do a fair amount of island hopping and jet-setting, sampling new tour offerings and the like.

Of course, many people travel for business as well as pleasure, and a lot of an agent's job is making arrangements for conferences, sales meetings and company trips. In addition to agencies, many corporations have their own in-house travel departments to handle the arrangements of getting 600 employees from 190 different locations to the same place at the same time. (Sometimes they can even arrange for their luggage to get there, too.)

In addition to corporate and agency travel careers, a great many people in the travel field work for tour operators, resorts, cruise lines and other independent providers. These are considered the really glamorous and exciting jobs in the industry, and it's easy to see why. What with travel to exotic ports of call, first-class flights around the

world, fabulous meals and sightseeing, you almost don't notice the
jet-lag, seasickness and assaults on your digestive system. I don't
know about you, but I could certainly live with a job as director of
the Club Med in Martinique. Okay, so there are a few bugs . . .

Any and all of these exciting careers are open to you with no more
than a high school degree and a strong stomach. There are airline
programs and independent travel schools which can help tremendously, and it's good to know some foreign languages. There are other
ways you can prepare,too, but let's look first at some of the many
different jobs in travel and their responsibilities.

——————————PEOPLE IN TRAVEL——————————

Probably the most visible travel professionals are agency travel
consultants, whose responsibilities are more varied and interesting
than many people realize. To begin with, travel agents do not collect
commissions or fees of any kind from clients. Their services are free
of charge to consumers. I am always amazed at how many people
insist on fouling up their own travel plans when there are so many
qualified travel agents who will make arrangements for them at no
cost. Travel arrangements are better left to travel professionals,
people who are paid by airlines, hotels and tour operators for filling
space in their lines.

Travel agents handle all kinds of arrangements for all kinds of
trips. Americans, it seems, can't get enough of the greener grass on
the other side. We have made travel a multi-billion dollar a year
industry. Agencies advertise the many tours and trips they offer in
local newspapers, magazines and on radio. Once you are interested
in a particular destination, they arrange all necessary transportation
and accommodations, explain what is included and what's not and
recommend places for the activities you're interested in, be it whale-
watching or mountain climbing. They also will give their clients a
good estimate of what the whole deal will cost. Many destinations
today are good bargains, but travelers do have to pay for some things
(like airline tickets) up front. You as a travel agent should explain
cancellation penalties, if any, and offer trip insurance.

As travel-happy as we all are, the bulk of an agency's business
comes not from tourists but corporations. Here the agent's job is not
so much recommending destinations as making sure employees
have rooms when they get there. Planning the arrangements for
hundreds of people attending a convention in Caracas can become a
three-ring circus if you don't know what you're doing. There are
always last-minute changes, and travel agents have to stay cool

under pressure. The manager in Minneapolis may have to change planes seven times, but you will get him to the hotel, where you must also make arrangements for banquets, sightseeing trips, entertainment and recreational activities. Many times these last responsibilities are turned over to the company's corporate travel department, which offers its own career demands and rewards.

Corporate travel people sometimes make transportation reservations, but usually they are more involved in taking care of the group once they get there. Depending on the type of trip, the company may require facilities for a budget meeting or a gourmet banquet. Corporate travel representatives negotiate with hotels for group room and meal rates, research available recreational activities and obtain special equipment like computer terminals, video monitors or snorkeling masks and fins.

It is also their responsibility to do it all within the company budget, which makes a large part of the job shopping around for the best values. Employees do a lot of individual business travel as well as convention going, and their arrangements must be made efficiently and economically. If an employee lays out any of his own money for travel expenses, he submits receipts for reimbursement. These are reviewed by those in the travel department, and expense checks are authorized.

Serving travel arrangers in both corporations and agencies are the travel providers; that is, the airlines and resorts, the tour and cruise operators and the many other businesses offering something to tourists and business travelers. While it is possible to book a trip or cruise as an individual, the vast majority of an operator's business is contracted through agencies and corporate travel people. Thus, the major focus of their advertising and marketing efforts is not the public but those professionals involved in making recommendations and arrangements.

There are really three different types of travel providers: airlines and other transportation companies, hotels and resorts, and independent operators. People in transportation work not only for the scheduled airlines like TWA and Pan Am, but for non-scheduled, or charter lines as well. Indeed, when the cost of air transportation is the largest expense of a planned trip, as it often is today, more and more people are turning to more economical charter flights to save money. Charter flights are called non-scheduled because they do not have scheduled take-off and landing times, or for that matter, flight paths. Their airports of departure and destination work them into the patterns between scheduled flights when time is available. Thus, take-off times and places for charter flights must be flexible, and the flight may be cancelled altogether if it is not fully subscribed. In that case, your client's money is refunded, but they, unfortunately, have lost their vacation.

Whether scheduled or charter, people in the airline industry work in the air (flight attendants) and on the ground, too (reservationists, ticketing agents, hospitality personnel). If you aspire to "fly the friendly skies," you either will have to attend a special airline school or go through a training program sponsored by a carrier to become licensed. Careers on the ground are usually learn as you go.

Travel professionals in hotels and other resorts are responsible for filling rooms, accommodating groups, arranging local transportation, directing guests to points of interest, chartering fishing boats, providing maps of the ruins of the ancient temples, recovering lost articles, locating a doctor in the middle of the night, preparing banquets, providing entertainment and doing a million other little things that will make a guest want to come back to Paradise Plantation. Of course, it's more than a one person effort, and careers include Sales, Banquet Management, Activities Director, Reservationist, and — that recent and welcome import from Europe — the Concierge, or hospitality director. The work can be demanding, but it's gratifying to work in an environment where your primary objective is to keep people happy. The fringe benefits of working at a place like the Acapulco Princess aren't bad, either.

Finally, there are many exciting jobs with independent tour and cruise operators. If you always have dreamed of hosting the captain's dinner on the Love Boat, this is the place for you. Unlike working for a resort, tour personnel may travel extensively, particularly if they work for one of the many special interest lines which are proliferating like rabbits. Today, almost any hobby or activity merits its own Global Tour, be it archaeological digging, auto racing, deep sea diving, bird watching, photography, cooking or bicycling. All of these tours employ a lot of very lucky people on site, including hospitality agents, activities directors, translators and tour managers. To my mind, this is the fun side of the travel business, and it pays well, too. It also is the most desirable, and therefore a very competitive area for travel jobs.

You cannot just walk into a position as tour director, or any other type of upper level travel work for that matter. There are, however, a variety of ways to break into travel, depending on where you live, where you want to end up and how selective you are.

Let's look at some entry level jobs and their responsibilities in the following section.

───────────── THE ENTRY LEVEL ─────────────

If you live near a major metropolitan airport, you may get into the business as a reservationist for one of the scheduled airlines. There is no special education required for this, though the airline will put you through its own training program before putting you in front of passengers. Of course, airline reservation systems are computerized now. In fact, it's hard to imagine how they managed before the age of automation. A large airline offers literally thousands of flights every day, each carrying hundreds of passengers to and from hundreds of destinations. It doesn't take a mathematical wizard to figure that it all adds up to millions of opportunities for things to go wrong —and sometimes they do. But on the whole, ticketing and other airline systems work remarkably well, thanks to well trained and patient reservationists.

Once you have completed your training, you will be put in charge of fielding passenger calls as well as handling reservations in person. Working with a world-wide computer system, you will check flight schedules and seat availability, process changes and cancellations and even recommend other carriers if your airline cannot accommodate a passenger's schedule. For all of this, you can expect to earn between $12,000 and $15,000 a year to start, more if reservationists are included in the union representing employees at your airline. In addition, most carriers offer their employees free travel, a very nice fringe benefit.

Sometimes you can get into travel through the corporate side, helping to plan conferences or make arrangements for company trips. Here you will be responsible for checking out prices, making airline and hotel reservations, distributing the necessary information to employees, etc. As an entry level corporate travel representative, you might make $12,000 to $14,000 a year, possibly more if you worked in the industry part-time or summers. This is not a very common place to start out, though, and you might be better off looking into local hotel work.

Even the smallest backwater town has a Holiday Inn or Best Western Motor Lodge, and you can start out there as a desk clerk/reservationist, banquet server or facilities manager. The pay in these positions is not great, somewhere between minimum wage and $12,000-$13,000 a year, but there are opportunities to move up once you are there. If you live in a tourist area, you may be in luck; you should be able to get in with a good resort. Otherwise, try to get into a large chain where you may have the chance to transfer to a larger hotel in a more desirable area.

If you want to fly United, for example, you'll have to pay for several months training at an airline school. Unless you live in a major city, you will also have to move. Be warned that a good percentage of students wash out of these programs; in fact, the schools plan for it. There are simply too many people and too few jobs for everyone to make it. I don't recommend starting out this way. But, if you do and you make it, the money is good, with first year earnings between $16,000 and $18,000 a year. Again, this is due to the unions, because the job just isn't that difficult, nor is there any shortage of personnel. Many airlines today are in serious financial trouble, though, and steward(ess) work is not the cushy, secure job it once was. Give-backs and layoffs are common in the industry today.

Prospects are somewhat better in the cruise industry, where you might sign on as a waiter or waitress, bartender, exercise instructor or hospitality person. Here again, entry level salaries aren't great, but who cares? Your expenses are minimal, with your employer providing food and shelter. You have days off, like any other job, and when you do, you're on a cruise ship, or in an exotic port.

When you are working, your responsibilities will vary with the job, but if you have any kind of expertise in an activity like ballroom dancing, aerobic exercise, cooking or ping-pong, you stand a good chance of landing a job as an activities aide. Here you will instruct groups of passengers in your specialty, get paid a little more for it and have a blast. If I were eighteen again, I'd do it in a minute.

What is the work environment like? It varies a lot depending on whether you work in a resort, on a ship or for an airline, but except for corporate travel, all of these employers are in service industries, and thus have a good deal in common. It pays to have the personality for this kind of work, because you will do a lot of little things to accommodate paying guests, some of which you may think totally unreasonable. Then, too, the hours are irregular, and some areas of the industry are very seasonal.

Most of all, you have to like people, because in the travel business, you're going to deal with all kinds, and I mean all kinds. A travel agent's client may change her travel plans seven times in three months. A hotel concierge may be asked to locate the nearest kosher restaurant (in Panama). Cruise directors must find alternate accommodations for passengers who "want to be nearer to the casino." Tourists can try the patience of an angel, and business travelers are not much better. Have you ever tried to find six overhead projectors at 8:00 a.m. on a Saturday?

The person who can remain calm in the face of pressure is highly valued in the travel industry. When you remember that, to the guest, her vacation may represent an entire year's savings as well as the only opportunity to get away from it all until next year, it's understandable that things like lost luggage, fully-booked golf courses and bad weather can be major disasters. There's not much you can do about the weather, of course, except maybe organize a bridge tournament, but there are a million little crises which you must resolve calmly and quickly. Travel just is not the place for those who are easily flustered, or who panic when the wrong flowers are delivered to their wedding.

If the travel industry appeals to you, there are many ways to go. Wherever you start out, the important thing is to get some experience under your belt. then go after what you really want. Let's look now at some of the typical career paths available to travel professionals.

CAREER PATHS

Probably the most visible travel professionals are those who work in agencies. Travel agents, or consultants, have a variety of responsibilities, and are paid for and judged by the amount of business they bring in. At first, of course, you will not have your own clientele, and you probably will take a lot of cold calls and serve drop-in customers. Most of your time will be spent reserving flights and hotel rooms, which in itself can be a Herculean task. Ever since deregulation, figuring out the cheapest way to get from A to B has become one big game. Why a flight from Buffalo to Baltimore requires three connections and costs more than flying coast to coast I don't know, but it does. A good travel agent can minimize transportation costs by knowing about and using Supersaver and excursion fares when available. As the ads say, "some restrictions apply," and a client may have to reserve a certain amount of time in advance, depart midweek, stay over a Saturday night and return on a "red eye." But there are ways to save, and it takes a while to learn the ins and outs of the system.

Once you have developed a customer base, you will start to get not only repeat business but referrals, too. By that point, you should have a pretty good understanding of what tours and special programs your agency sponsors, and can begin to make recommendations about where and when to go, where to stay, what to see and eat and what to avoid. Few tourists know, for example, that December is the rainiest month of the year in Florida. Most travel agents know, but since the Christmas vacation period is the busiest travel season, few tell their clients about it. However, you will soon learn that it is not enough to make a killing once around. It is the repeat business that provides a steady income, and you cannot afford to burn too many clients too often. Anyone who has spent a wet and miserable week in a Miami hotel room with three wet and miserable kids who can do nothing but complain about how wet and miserable they are is not likely to use your fine service a second time. If you're lucky, they won't tell their friends about you!

Travel agents are paid a combination of salary and commissions for the tour and airline space they sell. This is paid to them by the agency, which in turn collects from the hotels, airlines and tour operators. Theoretically, it is possible to make great money in travel, but in reality, it's a lot like real estate. The only ones who really make out are the agency principals. It's rare for even an experienced agent with a fantastically loyal clientele to make much over $20,000 a year. Most earn between $14,000 and $18,000. True, there are a lot of fringe benefits like agency-paid trips and the sheer fun of talking to hotel clerks in Bombay, but many people use their agency experience to land more lucrative jobs in the industry — like corporate travel representative, for example.

People in corporate travel necessarily are less concerned with making recommendations. Sure, Newport is quaint, but the Seattle office manager is going to Little Rock for a reason. Your job is to get him there in a reasonable amount of time for a reasonable amount of money. In some companies, employees pay their own way and submit expense reports for reimbursement. Recently a lot of companies have experienced problems with this system; namely, employees tend to fly hundreds of miles out of their way or pay more than they might to fly on a particular airline whose travel credits they are collecting for personal trips. And so, once again, reservations are being turned over to the travel departments.

In addition to arranging individual employee travel, corporate travel representatives are responsible for making all arrangements necessary for company meetings, industry conferences and trade shows. These involve the transport of all kinds of equipment as well as lots of people from lots of different places. Once you get them there, you have to meet them at the airport, wine and dine them at banquets, transport them to native bazaars, hire interpreters and guides and otherwise play host to the employees. Many of these services can be provided by the resort or hotel, but it is still up to the corporate travel people to do the price shopping, negotiate group rates and get everyone home in one piece.

Usually, corporate travel planners have some type of experience in the industry, be it agency or hotel background. Experienced corporate travel people are somewhat better paid than are agency consultants, and can earn $27,000-$28,000 or more in a large company. It is, however, undeniably less exotic work, but then, you'll be making enough to vacation on your own.

Careers with travel providers may be the most desirable of all. There are all kinds of jobs to suit all talents and tastes. Are you a congenial man-about-town? You may find your calling as a tour or cruise director, where you cordially greet guests as they arrive, graciously present an evening's entertainment, turn on the charm as you make the rounds of dinner guests and contribute a witty remark here and there.

Are you a born leader? The sort who could sell ice to the Eskimos? Consider a career as a marketing representative for a tour operator, resort or cruise line. You will be responsible for promoting the operator or resort to travel agents, corporate travel officers and the public at large. You will oversee the production and distribution of brochures, invite potential corporate clients and agency sponsors to sample your services, negotiate group rates and draw up and sign contracts with large clients. In a sales and marketing position, you are paid again a combination of salary and commission. It can add up to a substantial income of $30,000 a year or more.

Maybe you are a natural organizer. Your talents might best be utilized as host or ground manager for a tour operator. This kind of position involves less travel, which can be a welcome change from sleeping on four different continents every other week. Ground managers handle transportation and other arrangements for the tour group once they arrive at a particular destination. People are there to meet the group at the airport, buses or limousines are provided to take them to their hotels, guides are hired for sightseeing trips and local hosts are provided to escort the group on excursions, pointing out where Alexander the Great slept and other points of interest. Unlike tour directors, who travel with every group (and must get awfully tired of climbing the 100 or so steps leading to the Vatican), ground managers are permanently located in exciting places tourists want to visit. The hours are irregular, and the pace can be hectic, but a tour host can expect to earn $18,000-$25,000 a year or more, and may get to live on the Riviera.

Finally, many city and state governments, tired of listening to "I love New York," have beefed up their departments of tourism with promotional people, multi-lingual information representatives and convention and group tour resource people. These are all good travel careers with good pay, though a somewhat less romantic image. The work can nonetheless be exciting, with local tourism representatives involved in campaigns to attract to their area political conventions, major sporting events, industry trade shows and other commercial business. It's certainly a good alternative for home town men and women who like the travel business but not travel itself, and there are quite a few.

Whichever exciting area of this exciting field you choose, you probably will develop special expertise in one or another area of the business. Many travel agents, for example, specialize in business travel, catering exclusively to corporate and government clients. There are many advantages to this approach. For instance, an agent who works only with business clients becomes well known quickly and gets a lot of referrals. Then, too, practice makes perfect, and consultants who serve only one type of client are undoubtedly more knowledgable about the subtle ways and means of things.

Other agents specialize in group travel. Indeed, a great many large agencies own their own charter companies and represent them to their clients. This not only affords tremendous economies, it also ensures greater control over the whole show. From a customer's perspective, that can mean increased accountability. There is nothing more frustrating than having a bad experience become an even worse one, as travel agents, hotels, airlines and tour operators pass the buck among themselves. Agencies which specialize in group travel hopefully can avoid problems to begin with, due to their extensive experience with the arrangements and pitfalls peculiar to their industry. I mean, after so many years and so many Theater Weeks in London, everything that can go wrong already has. The agent should know how to prevent the same problems from reoccuring.

A newer and rapidly expanding travel market is the special interest tour, which by its very nature caters to a special clientele. Tour operators, resorts, even cruise ships have hopped on the bandwagon. The unwitting tourist may find himself booked into a tennis clinic in Puerto Rico, a cooking workshop in Lausanne or a Dude Ranch in Arizona. On the other hand, travelers with special hobbies can sign up for group excursions with like-minded people wishing to enjoy Fall Foliage, cross-country skiing, great art museums of the western world or salmon fishing.

At this point, you probably are ready to join the Merchant Marines to break into travel, but there are better and more practical ways to prepare for your career. Let's look at some of them now.

PREPARATION

From an educational perspective, there are two types of schools which can help prepare you for a career in travel: travel agent and flight attendant programs. If you are interested in the arranging end of the business, your best bet is to check out some travel agent schools in your area (there are a number of them spotted all over the country).

Generally, these programs require 3-9 months to complete, depending on whether you attend full or part-time. An adequate program should cost around $600 or $700, certainly not more than $1000. The most important training you will get at these schools will be on one or more types of airline computerized reservation systems. Several airlines have such systems, which are supposed to tell an agent the most economical flights available from and to anywhere anytime, regardless of the carrier. This is seldom the case (unless American really does have the cheapest fare every time). And like most computer systems, your answer depends on how the question is asked. Nonetheless, it is helpful to know how to use these systems, and it is a very big plus when you look for that first job. Although some agencies still provide their own training, most do not, and a good travel school can be an excellent investment.

The other type of education you may find useful is one from an airline flight school. There are two ways to go with this, the most common being to pay for training that is designed to prepare you for becoming licensed to work in the air. As mentioned earlier, even getting into these schools is very competitive, and the failure rate once you're in is quite high. Completing the program is by no means a guarantee that you will be licensed, nor is a license a sure ticket to a flight attendant job. If all of this sounds discouraging, I'm glad, because far too many people have a lot of delusions about the whole business, illusions some unscrupulous travel schools are only too happy to perpetuate. If your heart is really set on it, by all means, give it a whirl, but at least walk in with your eyes open.

A slightly different twist on flight attendant training is the airline-sponsored program. These, too, are extremely competitive, but here the airline picks up the tab for your training. While you are not technically an airline employee, and receive no salary, the big benefit here is that the airline has some commitment to you. They are motivated to see you succeed, and do everything possible to see that you do. One of the biggest believers in this system is People Express Airlines (Newark, NJ.) I'm sure there are others, and I would recommend this approach over a private travel school.

Not that any special schooling is needed at all for many travel careers. You even can get some practical work experience while you are still in high school. As a young teenager, you may have been sent on what is known in the industry as a "teen tour." Regardless of what you thought at the time, these tours offer a good opportunity to experience first-hand a lot of what you might do later on as a tour or cruise director. Sign up this summer as a counselor or host or guide, whatever they call them. Not only will it look good on your résumé, if you can live through two months in a Winnebago with 20 adolescents, shepherding middle-aged tour groups will be a piece of cake.

Another possibility is summer work on a cruise ship. If all you can find is housekeeping work, you might not get much out of it except a nice tan. However, as mentioned earlier, your expertise in some athletic or recreational area may land you an instructor's job. This is fabulous experience, and a good earning opportunity as well.

If you are not lucky enough to land either of the above summer "jobs," you might look into work at a local hotel or resort. This can even be done part-time during the school year, a good idea because it will put you ahead of everyone else when it's time to hire summer help. Consider not only working behind the desk but also in the sales office, banquet room, hospitality center and recreational facilities. As always, get references, and look up your old boss after graduation.

If you live in an area of even passing attraction to tourists, you should also look up your local Tourist Information Center. Because they are government agencies, they often have special programs which employ and train young people during the summer months. If nothing else, you'll be able to do some volunteer work. It's hard on the wallet, but volunteer experience is as good as any other, and it's better than nothing on your résumé.

However you get your start, a career in travel is unquestionably something out of the ordinary. The work is challenging, the environment exciting, the people fun-loving and the pay not bad. On top of that, it's an industry in which your lack of a degree is even less important than not having a current tetanus booster shot. The career potential is tremendous, and the careers themselves can only be described as wonderful. Sure, there is a lot of competition, but nothing worthwhile is easy. You have at least as good a shot as anyone else, better having read this. Now you know what it's all about and what you're up against, Bon Voyage!

11

The How-To Part

If you have read this far, you probably have gathered this is not a how-to book-for a lot of reasons. For one thing, there are more than enough good books out there on how to get a job. However, there were not any that I could find which described different careers in enough detail that an intelligent person could make an informed career choice.

So why a how-to section now, at the very end of the book? Well, there are some things peculiar to the non-degreed candidate's job search which bear discussion. Even the best books available are not really written for you, the high school graduate competing with the millions of degreed and/or more experienced applicants out there.

It's not easy deciding to go right into the business world after high school. For one thing, it's different (though becoming more popular by the day), and in high school, anything different is suspect. It's easy to feel left out when friends are caught up in the merry-go-round of SAT's, applications and waiting for that all-important envelope from that all-important college. Whatever your reasons are for not going to college, your last year in high school is sure to start you wallowing in self-pity and remorse. It will seem as though every person on the face of the earth except you is going to college. Your parents were right, you should have applied. You should have taken out a loan. You'll never amount to anything without a degree.

Baloney. You have just read about ten exciting and challenging careers you can pursue without sheepskin in hand, and they are by no means the only ones. Space prohibits listing all of the many options available to you at this point in your life. There is absolutely no reason to feel that your horizons are limited by your decision not to get a degree right now. On the other hand, your college-bound friends are feeling quite constrained if not downright trapped by the prospect of spending the next four or more years behind ivy covered walls, while the real world passes them by. So buck up and start getting ready for that all-important, all-exciting first job.

The first thing you need, of course, is a résumé. My Random House dictionary, which is the size of a small imported car and contains all the news that's fit to print, defines a résumé as "a brief account of personal, educational and professional qualifications, as of an applicant for a job." The operative word here is *brief*. If Lee Iacocca's résumé is a mere four pages, your qualifications, potentially dazzling as they may be, should require no more than one.

The one and only purpose of any résumé is to generate job interviews. No one ever hired a résumé, and if yours is going to create any interest at all it must be all of the following: neat, professional, organized and job-related. By neat, I don't mean just the absence of juice stains, although that's a definite plus. To look professional, your résumé must contain no errors of any kind. If you don't know how to spell a word, look it up. If you make a typing error, and it can't be fixed so that it is not noticeable, re-type the whole thing (remember, it's only one page). Photocopied résumés are fine, but be sure the copies aren't too dark or too light. A résumé reproduced on a mimeograph machine is not acceptable.

After appearance, the most important aspect of your résumé will be its format. The only charts in this book (pages 150-151) present two sample résumés (before and after, if you will). Notice that the applicant in both cases has given not only her address, but a daytime and evening phone number where she may be reached for further information or to arrange an interview. I can't tell you how many résumés I have received that neglected to include the applicant's phone number, Needless to say, they went right into the old circular file, as will yours if you forget to give contact information.

After the applicant's name and contact information you will see the heading *Objective* listed first. The "Before" résumé (Résumé A) indicates that the applicant wants a challenging position with a dynamic company where she can work with people and achieve maximum career growth. Aside from the fact that there are no such jobs, as an employer I have no idea whatsoever what kind of openings I might have to match her skills. Indeed, her objective is filled with everything she wants from my company, but makes no mention of what, let alone how, she will contribute to the company in return .

Résumé B, on the other hand, presents several actual jobs the applicant would like to have, as well as how and what she will contribute to the firm in such a position. Not only does this reflect a more professional attitude, it also saves the employer the trouble of having to figure out what jobs the rest of your résumé says you're qualified to do. As important as your job search is to you, your résumé is just another one of hundreds most large companies receive every day. The sooner you can grab an employer's attention, and the easier your résumé is to read, the better your chances of receiving further consideration.

Which is why the next section, summary of qualifications, is so important. This is your chance to say, in a nutshell, *what you can do.* Can you type? Use a computer? Read German? Juggle? Anything that might possibly be relevant to the type of job you want should be included here. The *Experience* and *Education* sections will allow you to elaborate on these things, so keep it short and sweet, but say it. A résumé is no place for modesty, false or otherwise. In the words of Mohammad Ali, "If you can do it, it ain't braggin.'" And so what if it is? No one else is going to toot your horn; it's up to you to put your achievements and qualifications in the best light.

While you're going for it, be sure also to relate your experience and education to real-world job skills and situations. It may be obvious to you that your two years as captain of the debate team, winner of an unprecedented two consecutive Baltimore Conference championships, establishes your credentials as an outstanding public speaker. Yet you need to take that extra step and show how your experience will contribute to your effectiveness as the XYZ Company's Expeditor. The same goes for what you present in the Education section. Say it loud and make it clear how specific classes have prepared you for specific job responsibilities.

The final section, *Personal Data,* has undone more than a few otherwise highly effective résumés. The things to include under *Personal Data* are very limited, and not everyone needs to include them all, but here is my list: birthdate, access to transportation (own car, whatever), willingness to relocate and date you are available to begin employment. That's it. Do not include physical characteristics, and photos are definitely out.

Lastly, notice that both résumés conclude with the sentence "References available upon request." There is no need to include written references with your résumé. If and when things develop further with a particular employer, he will request whatever references are needed at that time. You should, however, prepare your references now. Naturally you have collected written recommendations from former teachers and employers; in addition, most companies ask for phone numbers of people you are listing as references. Common courtesy, not to mention self-interest, requires that you ask these people beforehand if you may use them as references. They will be flattered. If you don't ask, and they get a phone call

Résumé A

Lynn Miller
409 Academy Circle
Leola, MA 06061
(H) 617-555-1212
(W) 617-555-2222

OBJECTIVE:

To obtain a challenging position in administration with a dynamic company where I can work with people and achieve maximum career growth.

QUALIFICATIONS:

3.6 GPA; part-time work experience for Hartford Insurance Corp; Class Vice-President.

EXPERIENCE:

Temporary clerk position with Hartford Insurance, Summer, 1984. Answered telephones, filed claim forms, typed reports and expedited policies from state capitol.

Part-time receptionist for Dewey, Takum and Howe, 1983-1984. Answered phones, scheduled appointments and performed general office duties.

EDUCATION:

Diploma from Leola High School, June 1985. General Studies.

PERSONAL INFORMATION:

Birthdate: 6/20/67
Health: Excellent
Hobbies: Tennis, cooking, astrology, and collecting Civil War memorabilia.

REFERENCES AVAILABLE UPON REQUEST.

Résumé B

Lynn Miller
409 Academy Circle
Leola, MA 06061
(H) 617-555-1212
(W) 617-555-2222

OBJECTIVE:

Challenging position in Customer Relations, Loan Processing or related area where I can utilize my strong figure aptitude and computer skills to the company's best effect.

QUALIFICATIONS:

Excellent data entry and computer operation skills; type 50 wpm; good mathematical aptitude; well organized; good communication skills.

EXPERIENCE:

Summer 1984 - Hartford Insurance Corp., Brownsville, MA. Responsible for handling customer inquiries over the phone, assisting customers with claim forms an procedures, cutting through red tape to expedite insurance cards from state government offices. Also filled in for bookkeeper on maternity leave, preparing monthly statements and issuing invoices. All of Hartford Insurance's systems were automated, and I became very familiar with data entry and computer operations. Offered full-time position, which I had to decline due to continuing education.

Summer 1983 and 1983-84 school year - Business Manager for Leola High School Thespian Society. Complete financial responsibility for all Society activities. Planned fund raising projects, recorded all transactions, authorized and monitored expenses, balanced checking account statements and ledger. Managed business operation for Summer Theater and two school year productions, spending less money than in previous year.

EDUCATION:

Graduate of Leola High School, Leola, MA. Maintained 3.6 grade average. Pursued special studies in business related courses, including business math, economics, and accounting. Also completed three advanced computer courses.

PERSONAL DATA:

Birthdate: 6/20/67
Date Available: Immediately
Open to relocation

REFERENCES AVAILABLE UPON REQUEST.

out of the blue, they will be flustered. This is bound to reflect badly on you. It will annoy the people you list as references, too.

So. There you sit, résumé in hand, ready to take on the world of work. Where will you send this important document? It never fails to amaze me how many people overlook the most obvious and potentially productive places to apply, namely, their former employers. Did you work part-time for a department store? Serve an internship with the Office of Tourism? Do artwork for a local dinner theater production? Look up those people for whom you did work of some consequence. Let them know you are now out of school and looking for full-time employment. I can't emphasize enough how much better your chances are of getting in somewhere you are known, rather than some company where yours is just another face in the crowd (or more likely a name; you may never get your face in the door). Even if old employers don't have any work available, they may know someone who does, and a personal recommendation is the best introduction you can get.

After you have touched base with former employers, contact everyone you have ever known. Let them know you are looking for a job, and what kinds in particular you are qualified for. A lot of people are hesitant about approaching acquaintances about job opportunities, as if being unemployed should make them too humble to speak with Employers. This seems especially to be true when the acquaintances are friends of one's parents. Rest assured that those acquaintances have children of their own, and will push them to talk to your parents about a job when the time comes. It is a ritual in which all parents participate, starting when their children suddenly refuse to mow the lawn anymore because Mr. Lafferty is paying them $10 to do his. Ask everyone you know; it is not an imposition. In fact, most people will be flattered, and if you can put up with a little "free advice," you may get some good job leads.

The next place to look is your local library, which has an Industrial Directory of all the employers in your town, describing what they do, number of employees and names of people in important positions. Copy the names and addresses of all those companies which you think might hire people to do the kind of work you want to do. Then go to those companies and apply for a job. In person. Yes, you could just send a résumé, but that is what all of the degreed and experienced applicants are doing. Your goal is to stand out in the crowd. By bothering to apply in person, your résumé will be more likely to get into a tickler file somewhere instead of the circular one. This is because it will be attached to the company's application. For whatever reason, people do not like to throw away their own company forms. They look official. They cry out to be copied, distributed or filed or something. When an opening next comes up, and they do regularly, your "paperwork" will be there first, before the flood of résumés sure to come in if the company advertises the position. Many don't advertise, which is why help-wanted ads are low on the list of places to look for a job. Nonetheless, they are *on* the list, and there are ways to use these ads to the best effect.

The first thing to know about help wanted ads is that they are written by employers looking to hire a cross between Clark Kent and Superman — humble and cheap, yet hugely overqualified. The fact is, if such ideal applicants exist, they are unlikely to be challenged by the job offered. Thus if you can claim to satisfy even 30% of a job's "required qualifications," send out your résumé. This also goes for ads which specify that candidates must be degreed. Remember your "equivalent experience," and send that résumé — with a cover letter.

A good cover letter will personalize the information given in your résumé. Naturally every job is different, and you cannot write a new résumé for every position you might fit. If a certain skill is emphasized in the ad, your cover letter can highlight relevant aspects of your experience not elaborated upon in your résumé. Always address the letter to a name, not Personnel Manager or Dear Sir or Madam. If the ad gives only a P.O. box and no company or individual name, don't apply. That "once in a lifetime opportunity to break into real estate" is more than likely a job selling aluminum siding door-to-door.

As a last resort, you may be considering going to an employment agency. Don't. There are two kinds of agencies — ones where the employer pays the fee, and ones where you pay. The first, called "fee-paid" agencies, are not at all interested in you. They are paid by employers to find qualified applicants for positions the employers cannot fill themselves. Almost always, these are highly specialized jobs like Weapons Systems Engineers, Tax Attorneys or Pharmaceutical Products Sales Managers. They are never entry level, for the obvious reason that no employer needs to pay for the kind of person who walks into his personnel office every day. Alas, at this point in your life, you are in that category. You will waste not only the employment counselor's time but your own by going to his office.

The kind of employment agencies where you pay the fee are interested in you all right, but for the wrong reasons. Their goal is to put you in a job, any job, in order to collect from you. They rarely have any regard for what *you* want, and many of them are unscrupulous to boot. They usually prey on the desperate and the unemployed, making a lot of promises and producing little. Avoid them, and for heaven's sake, never sign anything with them.

At this point I think congratulations are in order. You have put together a good résumé, distributed it widely, called all your parents' friends and have no doubt generated quite a few interviews. I'm not going to go into how to interview; there are many books on that subject. But in your particular situation, that is, with no real experience or degree, you are bound to be asked something like "how entry level a position are you willing to take to start?" Often another way this can be put is "how's your typing?" This is a thorny issue for fresh graduates.

A lot of the careers in this book, like travel and publishing, are highly competitive. Even degreed candidates in such fields often begin as "gofers," and if you want to be considered for more professional positions, your best bet may be to take what you can get and work from the inside, as it were. In this case, at least be sure to get in with a reputable company, and don't allow yourself to be exploited. If you are doing editorial work, even after hours, you should get paid for it. When higher level positions open up, you (and your fellow "gofers") should be the first considered.

On the other hand, in an area like finance or data processing, you need to start out at the highest level possible. In the corporate mentality, once a data entry clerk, always a data entry clerk. Even if you could make more money starting in the secretarial pool (don't laugh), apply instead for positions like assistant bookkeeper or computer operator. Do not let employers sell you short because you lack formal training; keep looking until you find someone willing to give you the chance to show how prepared your own initiative and experience have made you.

Finally, I would advise you to look the part. You are no longer in high school, and would do well to look as professional as possible. This means not only investing in a small business wardrobe, but taking a critical look at your hairstyle, hands, nails and overall appearance. A short, neat cut is best for both male and female applicants (within reason). Trade in your three ring binders and notebooks for a good clipboard or portfolio, and definitely go for a solid, simple briefcase or attaché. You cannot help your youthful look, but doing everything possible to appear mature and professional will dramatically improve your employment prospects. You will be less nervous, too, sitting in a personnel waiting room if you at least fit in with your older competition.

And that is exactly what they are — older. For careers in the fields presented here as well as many others, they are no better qualified than you, except for one thing. Pay attention to that man behind the curtain:

> "Where I come from, we have great universities, seats of wisdom and learning, where people do nothing but sit and think deep thoughts. And they haven't any more brains than you have. But, they do have one thing you haven't got — a diploma. And so, by the authority vested in me by the state of Nebraska, ceteris paribus e pluribus unum, I hereby confer upon you the degree of Doctor of Thinkology".

There. Now you are just as qualified. And that's no B.S.

Index

[157]